JOHN PAIZS'S

CRIME WAVE

John Paizs's "Crime Wave" examines the Winnipeg filmmaker's 1985 cult film as an important example of early postmodern cinema and as a significant precursor to subsequent postmodern blockbusters, including the much more recent Hollywood film *Adaptation*. *Crime Wave*'s comic plot is simple: aspiring screenwriter Steven Penny, played by Paizs, finds himself able to write only the beginnings and endings of his scripts, but never (as he puts it) "the stuff in-between." Penny is the classic writer suffering from writer's block, but the viewer sees him as the (anti)hero in a film told through a stylistic parody of 1940s and 50s B-movies, TV sitcoms, and educational films.

In *John Paizs's "Crime Wave,"* writer and filmmaker Jonathan Ball offers the first book-length study of this curious Canadian film, which self-consciously establishes itself simultaneously as following, but standing apart from, American cinematic and television conventions. Paizs's own story mirrors that of Steven Penny: both find themselves at once drawn to American culture and wanting to subvert its dominance. Exploring Paizs's postmodern aesthetic and his use of pastiche as a cinematic technique, Ball establishes *Crime Wave* as an overlooked but important cult classic.

(Canadian Cinema)

JONATHAN BALL teaches courses in literature, film, and writing at the University of Manitoba and the University of Winnipeg.

CANADIAN CINEMA 11

JOHN PAIZS'S

CRIME WAVE

JONATHAN BALL

UNIVERSITY OF TORONTO PRESS
Toronto Buffalo London

tiff.

Toronto Buffalo London
utppublishing.com

ISBN 978-1-4426-4812-8 (cloth)
ISBN 978-1-4426-1617-2 (paper)

Publication cataloguing information is available from Library and Archives Canada.

TIFF and the University of Toronto Press acknowledge the financial assistance to its publishing program of the Canada Council for the Arts and the Ontario Arts Council.

Canada Council for the Arts Conseil des Arts du Canada

ONTARIO ARTS COUNCIL
CONSEIL DES ARTS DE L'ONTARIO
50 YEARS OF ONTARIO GOVERNMENT SUPPORT OF THE ARTS

This book has been published with the help of a grant from the Canadian Federation for the Humanities and Social Sciences, through the Awards to Scholarly Publications Program, using funds provided by the Social Sciences and Humanities Research Council of Canada.

University of Toronto Press acknowledges the financial support of the Government of Canada through the Canada Book Fund for its publishing activities.

Contents

To begin and then end – it makes me fall out of favor with myself. The sky full of false surmises, the desert empty: I only exist elsewhere. Tell me what it is that you know about me, because you seem to think that I can save myself … In the rain, the street lamps empty their pockets of change.

Jenny Boully, *The Book of Beginnings and Endings*

I real ly did mean to be good.

Steven Penny's last words (as typewritten), *Crime Wave*

Acknowledgments

This book could not exist without John Paizs, who has been generous with his time and materials and whose accomplishments deserve the highest praise. Thanks to Bethany Berard, David Navratil, Patrick Short, George Toles, Gene Walz, and Darren Wershler, for help or conversation at various stages of this project. Thanks to Dave Barber, Monica Lowe, and everyone at the Winnipeg Film Group, for help and support. Thanks to Kaylen Hann, for refusing to believe. Thanks to Siobhan McMenemy and everyone at the University of Toronto Press, and to the series editors, Bart Beaty and Will Straw, for making this book a reality through their hard work and encouragement. Thanks to my anonymous peer reviewers, for their strong suggestions. Thanks to Mandy Heyens and Jessie Taylor, as always, and to my family and friends for their continued support.

In his collection of interviews with Guy Maddin, Caelum Vatnsdal writes: "The work of John Paizs ... will no doubt one day be subjected to a laudatory rediscovery by the cinetelligensia."[1] Let us hope that day comes. I owe thanks to Vatnsdal, Maddin, Pevere, Cagle, and all of the other writers, artists, and fans who have kept interest in Paizs's films alive, and thus made possible my own interest, and the writing of this book.

JOHN PAIZS'S

CRIME WAVE

1

The Top! Few Films Made It!

In a sad but fitting testament to the neglect of John Paizs's *Crime Wave* (1985), when I announced to friends my plan to write this book they agreed the premise would make for a fine experimental novel (one masquerading as a work of academic non-fiction), which might even fool a few poor saps into believing the film existed. Even after my explanations and denials, one friend still refused to believe that I had not fabricated both Paizs and the film as an elaborate hoax. She remains impressed that I have (so she believes) faked the Wikipedia entry on *Crime Wave* without it being removed by some vague authority, due to its bizarre description of the film (in particular, its "flute and glockenspiel-based score").[1] I hope that, if nothing else, the appearance of this book persuades her.

On one hand, such professions of bad faith speak to the cleverness of Paizs's film. Over a quarter of a century has passed since *Crime Wave* debuted at the Festival of Festivals (later renamed the Toronto International Film Festival), yet the central conceit of *Crime Wave* can still strike audiences as cutting-edge. On the other hand, such reactions attest to the film's near-disappearance. Seventeen years after *Crime Wave*, *Adaptation* (2002) – also a metafiction about a screenwriter struggling to craft a script for the very film the audience is watching – would go on to win Academy Awards. Meanwhile, the ground-breaking *Crime Wave* languishes in obscurity. *Adaptation*'s Donald Kaufman, despite being a fictional character, garnered an actual Oscar nomination for Adapted Screenplay, but John Paizs remains known to few filmgoers.

Geoff Pevere writes that "*Crime Wave* may be the brightest treasure this country ever buried,"[2] and Robert L. Cagle notes that "John Paizs is Canadian cinema's forgotten child."[3] Paizs's short film *Springtime in Greenland* (1981) has been called "Canada's first ... postmodern film,"[4] but even if one contests this claim, Paizs's work remains exemplary of trends in postmodern film. The lamentable neglect of Paizs's oeuvre, especially his 1980s films, also belies their significance within Canada's cinema history. A central figure in the early days of the Winnipeg Film Group, Paizs was "the first filmmaker associated with the Winnipeg Film Group to reject the traditionally prescribed role of the 'prairie filmmaker' and begin to forge a unique stylistic identity."[5] Paizs is also notable for his influence on other, better-known filmmakers: Will Straw reports that "[Guy] Maddin claims that his interest in making movies ... was born at a screening of *The Obsession of Billy Botski* (1980), an early short film by fellow Winnipegger John Paizs."[6]

Paizs, together with Maddin, was responsible for bringing the work of the Winnipeg Film Group to national and international acclaim. Although Paizs may have faded from prominence, his direct influence persists within Winnipeg's still-productive film community, where Paizs remains a touchstone. Writing in 2009, Solomon Nagler argued that in the 1990s, "a group of Winnipeg filmmakers resisted ... the post-modern prairie aesthetic that surged in the Winnipeg Film Group in the late 1980s, where awkward suburban angst and whimsical dream logic peripatetics reigned with the works of John Paizs, and later Guy Maddin."[7] The term "prairie postmodernism," which Nagler alludes to, was coined by Pevere to label Paizs's own aesthetic.[8] The term now refers to a range of works by Maddin and other members of the Winnipeg Film Group, cementing the central place of Paizs in Winnipeg's pantheon.

Maddin, due to his continued success and activity since the 1980s, has earned an international profile and displaced Paizs as the patron saint of Winnipeg film. When Paizs is mentioned, it's often in the same breath as Maddin, unsurprising since the two were friends around the time of Paizs's 1980s productions and the beginning of Maddin's career. Thus, while Maddin's reputation has eclipsed Paizs's own, it's easy to forget that it was once Maddin who worked in the shadow of Paizs. Maddin's first film, *The Dead Father* (1985), completed in the same year as *Crime Wave,* bears some resemblance to Paizs's earlier films through its appropriation of outmoded cinematic styles (Maddin reaches further back than Paizs), peculiar narration, mannered acting, and absurdist dry humour. Notwithstanding similarities, Maddin has never been an imitator of Paizs, despite a seeming return, with *My Winnipeg* (2007), to the ironic pseudo-documentary format that Paizs mastered (and that Maddin both alters and extends in his self-described "docu-fantasia"). If things had gone better for *Crime Wave,* or if Paizs had not stopped writing and directing his own films after its completion, perhaps Paizs's name might be as familiar to cinephiles as Maddin's own.

Curiously, *Crime Wave* seems to anticipate its own failure to succeed in the cultural marketplace: Peter Vesuwalla notes that "on the surface it seems somehow prophetically autobiographical."[9] *Crime Wave* being the story of an independent filmmaker, Steven Penny, and his failed attempts to produce a breakout feature film, it's easy (perhaps too easy) to see Penny as a stand-in for Paizs. Paizs and Penny are equated throughout the film in a number of ways, from Paizs performing as Penny down to the initial "P" in their last names. Penny's penchant for "color crime movies" (a semi-fictional genre related to lurid 1950s noir, judging from the posters in Steven's apartment) leads him to labour over the script for "Crime Wave," which he intends to be the greatest color crime movie ever made. (Throughout this book I enclose "Crime Wave" in quotation marks when referring to Steven Penny's dreamed film-within-a-film, and present *Crime Wave* in italics when referring to the work of John Paizs – although the reader should understand that such clean separation cannot be maintained. Although it is pragmatic to distinguish *Crime Wave* from "Crime Wave," in a sense *Crime Wave* argues their equation, even as it also demands that the creation of "Crime Wave" be considered an impossible feat, not achievable even within fantasy.) Steven Penny suffers from a peculiar form of writer's block: he can write beginnings and endings but has trouble with middles, "the stuff in-between." As *Crime Wave* progresses, we are treated to different beginnings and endings (and discarded middles) from Steven's various scripts for "Crime Wave."

Steven Penny's protracted failure to complete "Crime Wave" also seems prophetic of *Crime Wave*'s fall into obscurity (the film remains unavailable today except as a bootleg, and was never officially released except as a now-rare VHS). It is easy to think of Paizs as a real-world Penny, his career obstructed not by psychotic script doctors (see below) but by an uncaring industry incapable of recognizing *Crime Wave*'s artistry. However, Paizs did not fall victim to writer's block in the wake of *Crime Wave*'s completion, although he was unable to get subsequent projects off the ground before settling into a career as a director-for-hire. Although he no longer writes his own material, he continues to direct in this capacity, and also works as Director-in-Residence at the Canadian Film Centre.

Moreover, despite their relative obscurity, Paizs's 1980s films continue to garner interest and bear influence. Bruce McDonald has spoken of *Crime Wave* as "the first Canadian film I loved,"[10] and two of Paizs's short films (*The Obsession of Billy Botski* and *Springtime in Greenland*) have been re-released over the past decade as part of a DVD series of seminal films produced by the Winnipeg Film Group. John Kozak has identified Paizs as a vanguard figure in Canada's film history:

> Though the Winnipeg Film Group [since its founding in 1974] had been diligently exercising its mandate to support and promote independent filmmakers, those with the entrepreneurial spirit who initially took advantage of this unique opportunity largely took their cue from the National Film Board, and specialized in documentary, animation and the occasional experimental film ... And although the Winnipeg Film Group provided the infrastructure to support independent filmmaking, the spirit of a true independent film ideology, in the manner of David Lynch or Jim Jarmusch, did not yet exist in Manitoba. This would have to wait for the right filmmaker to come along with a highly personal vision to fully exploit this opportunity. This was the contribution John Paizs made, not just to the Winnipeg Film Group, but to a certain degree to Canadian filmmaking in general.[11]

This concept of a "true independent film ideology" seems problematic, doubly so given that such sentiments usually express an anti-Hollywood bias whereas Paizs's films have a more ambiguous relationship to Hollywood cinema. Moreover, insofar as this statement seems nationalistic, Maddin might be a better example, given his success. Kozak's sense of Paizs as an entrepreneur of sorts, whose early and artistic successes served as an important example for other local and national filmmakers and also constituted a break of sorts with the aesthetic and narrative concerns of Hollywood or Canadian faux-Hollywood features, bears more weight. Again, however, there is the problem of Paizs's aesthetic indebtedness to Hollywood (although to its cast-offs rather than its classics), and the fact that Maddin might be said to occupy this position instead, despite arriving later.

In any case, my goal in this book is to develop Kozak's sense of Paizs as a significant progenitor of work that still has not received its proper due, rather than pit Maddin versus Paizs in a cage match. I hope to redress a paucity of scholarship on Paizs: his extant critical attention consists of a mere handful of (often informal) articles, interviews, and reviews. Many of these publications are surveyed in chapter 2, which places *Crime Wave* in the broader contexts of its production, its reception, and John Paizs's filmography. That chapter also analyses Paizs's other 1980s films, which are discussed in some detail, since they prefigure the themes and aesthetics of *Crime Wave* and introduce and develop the "quiet man" character who becomes Steven Penny.

What I Mean By "Twists"

To ease analysis, *Crime Wave* might be divided into four loose sections, or "acts." In its first act, *Crime Wave*'s metafictional conceit is established as Steven Penny writes, and the film presents, three different beginnings and endings to "Crime Wave." At the same time, Steven befriends a young girl, Kim, who narrates the story of Steven's struggle to write "Crime Wave." In the second act, after Steven stops writing in despair, this frame narrative occupies centre stage as Kim attempts to help Steven overcome his writer's block. She enlists the help of another screenwriter, Dr C. Jolly, and Steven leaves Winnipeg for Sails, Kansas, to meet with this "script doctor." The third act concerns Steven's exploits in an unreal Kansas. Unbeknownst to Steven, Dr Jolly has become a serial killer – the selfsame kind of plot twist that this "doctor" prescribed as the cure-all to Steven's screenwriting ills. At his dire meeting with Dr Jolly, Steven is crushed by a street light. Instead of dying, Steven and his new street-light helmet transport back to Kim's Winnipeg bedroom, where Steven finds he has gained the magical power to write a final beginning and ending for "Crime Wave." The film's fourth act presents this final beginning and ending, a metafictional fantasy about "Steven Penny" soaring to stardom after writing and directing a string of Hollywood-styled blockbusters (in an attempt to clarify the tangled metafictional world of the film, I enclose "Steven Penny" in quotation marks when discussing the film-within-a-film character authored by Steven Penny). *Crime Wave* then ends with Kim's assurance that everything will end happily, since she has managed to write a middle for Steven's "Crime Wave," which concerns his struggle to write "Crime Wave," which suggests that *Crime Wave* is therefore "Crime Wave" (despite the fact that "Crime Wave" was supposed to be a "color crime movie" while *Crime Wave* is a comedic art film in a pseudo-documentary format).

Strange though its plot may sound, as Pevere observes, "despite its angular digressions, movie-within-a-movie-within-a-movie conceits and obstinate refusal to settle into any singular narrative groove, *Crime Wave* [remains] inescapably a coherent work."[12] Its metafictional structure might seem at first glance like a narrative gimmick or hollow postmodern flourish, but as Maddin writes, "Paizs has devised a story framework which can support almost any number of gags and digressions, stories within the story. The digressions however are not merely strung out in a line like laundry; they either echo one another or build upon each other. Eventually the different characters from the separate subscripts interact, first with each other, then with Steven himself. The result is an exhilaratingly complex narrative, one with which you feel you can never quite catch up."[13]

I attempt, nonetheless, to "catch up" with *Crime Wave*'s narrative, by way of an extended analysis that considers each of its scenes in order while constructing a series of arguments en route to its end. This manner of close reading seems most sensible, given the twin purposes of this book: to afford scholarly consideration to an undervalued film, and to broaden exposure for a film that remains more or less unavailable at the time of this writing. My desire has been to craft a volume that can be read, understood, and enjoyed by those who have never seen the film (but let's hope this book also increases the possibility of *Crime Wave*'s restoration and reissue in some form). This method of exhaus-

Kim Brown (Eva Kovacs), with "color crime" movie posters in the background. Courtesy of John Paizs, from the director's personal collection.

tive exegesis seems in line with the film's own obsessive self-interest. Digressive analysis also seems appropriate for a pastiche film of disparate forms and styles. The perversity of taking such a rigorous look at an almost unwatched film is meant to constitute a form of radical redress for *Crime Wave*'s critical neglect, and an ironic overinvestment that mimics Paizs's own devoted mimicry of obscure and forgotten films.

This book likewise falls into four rough sections. First, this introductory chapter, having already introduced the reader to John Paizs and *Crime Wave*, next lays out my theoretical edifice. I cordon off and move through my argument's theoretical basis in this early chapter for a few reasons. The Canadian Cinema series presents its volumes to both a general and a specialist audience, and to avoid saturating the present volume with theory, in the interest of presenting a readable analysis, I do the heavy lifting early on. This allows for a later, more focused discussion of the film itself. At the same time, a separate chapter allows for greater focus on the relevant theory (a discussion I will continue to develop as the chapters unfold).

The second section of the book (chapter 2) provides further information on Paizs himself, the 1980s films that he produced prior to *Crime Wave* (which are worthy of their own volume, and which have a close relationship to *Crime Wave*, as we shall see), and the production and initial reception of *Crime Wave*. Aspects of the film's production will be discussed on occasion throughout the later chapters, but chapter 2 focuses primarily on the historical fact of the film and its material context.

The book's third section (chapters 3 to 7) develops my close reading of *Crime Wave*. Chapter 3 is the most exhaustive of these four, for two reasons: one, this first "act" is denser than those following, since it encloses three of Steven Penny's failed beginnings and endings to "Crime Wave"; and two, when fundamental aspects of the film's narrative and Paizs's aesthetic approach first become apparent, they warrant fuller explication. I describe the film as I present my analysis, since many readers will not have seen and indeed may never see this obscure film that deserves close, recuperative attention. Chapters 3 to 6 present and analyse the four rough "acts" of the feature film, while chapter 7 serves as a coda for this reading, in which I examine the original, alternative ending of *Crime Wave*.

The fourth and final section of this book (chapter 8) expands on the fundamental reason for its appearance in the Canadian Cinema series: *Crime Wave* is a significant Canadian cultural artefact, a neglected Canadian film that deserves greater critical attention – one that also stands as a commentary on Canadian culture itself and the spectral figure of Canadian identity that so often occupies cultural discussions.

John Paizs's 1980s films, which culminate with *Crime Wave*, display a particularly postmodern aesthetic through their practice of pastiche, a technique of copying that Paizs uses to reproduce the forms and styles of paracinematic, "trash" cinema. Paizs's pastiche and his related forms of copying mark *Crime Wave* as exemplary of particular trends in postmodern film; furthermore, the specific way that the metafictional content of *Crime Wave* unfolds, and the unusual figure of the "quiet man" that Paizs copies from short film to short film to *Crime Wave*, develop "copying" from an aesthetic approach into something suggestive of a model for subject formation. The protagonists of Paizs's films are driven by fantasies that are themselves copied from elsewhere, and as Paizs's technique of copying is generative rather than degenerative, so Steven Penny's impossible fantasy is the basis for his identity as a "quiet man" – an identity that has been "copied" from Paizs's earlier films and transplanted to *Crime Wave*.

Crime Wave thus takes up an ambivalent, self-reflexive position relative to its own postmodernity, even as Steven Penny writes "Steven Penny" into "Crime Wave" in a way that posits the self as Other. In its narrative development and structural form, the film displays postmodern qualities yet transcends the particular context of 1980s postmodernism.

Crime Wave accomplishes this through its impossible claim to be Steven's dreamed film "Crime Wave," while displacing this fantasized film (suggesting throughout that "Crime Wave" could never exist). The fantasy of creating "Crime Wave" produces *Crime Wave*, a film that nevertheless draws attention to its own failure to live up to this dreamed ideal.

Copying and difference are important parts of Paizs's aesthetic approach, but also important concepts in both postmodern theory contemporary with *Crime Wave*'s production and current cultural theory. Although worlds apart in other respects, the approaches of postmodern theorists like Jameson and Hutcheon and psychoanalytic theorists like Lacan and Žižek both usefully frame a discussion of *Crime Wave*, due to its unusually anxious approach to its own postmodernism. *Crime Wave* also suggests, in its themes and through its form, a particular Canadian posture relative to the United States and its cultural products (which Paizs copies, celebrates, and critiques, often in the same gesture). Thus John Paizs's *Crime Wave* deserves rediscovery not only for its artistry but also because it stands as uniquely Canadian in a non-stereotypical way, rooting a concept of identity within a method of copying that plays out in Paizs's filmic techniques, aesthetic approach, and metafictional story and structure.

The Crime (Wave) of Copying

Paizs's aesthetic approach of "copying" the surfaces and tropes of other types of films constitutes the most distinctive quality of his filmmaking style. Indeed, as Marcus Boon writes, "style [itself] is a way of copying, a way of imitating, and it is this way which can be said to be original."[14] Although Paizs's copying has multiple incarnations, most prevalent is his formal approach of copying the surfaces of various paracinemas (aping the look of "junk" cinemas such as television commercials, educational films, and lurid B-movies): a stylistic practice of pastiche.

Fredric Jameson identifies the artistic technique of pastiche as "one of the most significant features or practices in postmodernism today,"[15] and although Jameson's "today" then meant 1982, pastiche remains a common technique in postmodern art. Jameson defines pastiche as "like parody, the imitation of a peculiar or unique style, the wearing of a stylistic mask, speech in a dead language: but it is a neutral practice of such mimicry, without parody's ulterior motive, without the satirical impulse, without laughter, without that still latent feeling that there exists something normal compared with which what is being imitated is rather comic."[16] Here Jameson goes too far (humour exists in pastiche apart from satire and parody), but he does capture the sense that in pastiche the "copying" of style often seems "neutral" rather than value-loaded as in parody. A better way to distinguish pastiche from parody might be to consider the former, in Paizs's hands most of all, as an ambivalent practice of mimicry, without parody's clear motive.

Linda Hutcheon distinguishes parody and pastiche differently: for her, "forms like pastiche ... stress similarity rather than difference."[17] Hutcheon sees parodic forms operating to "seek differentiation in [their] relationship[s] to [their] model[s]; pastiche operates more by similarity and correspondence."[18] For Hutcheon, parody is often "without laughter," like Jameson's pastiche; also, Hutcheon's "parody requires [a] critical ironic difference"[19] that distinguishes it from pastiche (which may still be a tool of parody). Paizs's work does not often qualify as "parody" under this definition, since his ironic distance often serves not to critique but to celebrate the copied forms (their repetition is a method of enjoyment). In Paizs's work, critical ironic distance is usually established relative not to that which is copied, but to the technique of copying itself. Paizs's pastiche does not parody its copied forms so much as trouble or draw attention to the act of copying.

Pastiche, through its neutral repetition, emphasizes surfaces and the act of copying; by contrast, the critique-laden mimicry of parody takes up a position relative to that which is copied. Pastiche thereby aligns with postmodernism's generalized loss of faith in essences, which themselves bolster capitalist concepts of possession and exchange. For Boon, after postmodernism, "any discussion of property, intellectual or otherwise, must begin with this basic recognition: in any society, what I consider to be mine can be taken away – because ultimately nothing is mine, nothing belongs to me, and finally there is no me."[20] Of course, for Jameson this is precisely how "postmodernism replicates or reproduces – reinforces – the logic of consumer capitalism."[21] Through its destruction of concepts such as essence, postmodern thought frees otherwise stable notions like identity itself to become consumer products. (Indeed, the title of Jameson's essay "Postmodernism, or The Cultural Logic of Late Capitalism" suggests that postmodernism does not just "reinforce" such logic but *is* that logic. The "significant question," for Jameson and others, "is whether there is also a way in which [postmodernism and its techniques] resists that logic."[22])

Jameson's perceived lack of a "still latent feeling that there exists something normal" might be transmuted into an anxious lack, a still latent feeling that there exists "something" beyond the copy – something apart from imitable forms, an accessible reality that might be directly represented without collapsing into these forms. Boon argues that much of the anxiety that surrounds copying as a cultural practice stems from how copying undermines the concept of essence (if a thing can be copied, rather than mimicked, then it has no essential nature). Since, as Boon notes, "essence is a potent myth, one of the phantasmatic structures that allows mimetic figuration to take place,"[23] copying produces anxiety insofar as it threatens that myth. This is the anxiety that plagues a theorist of copying like Jean Baudrillard (who seems nevertheless ambivalent, writing in a tone of horrified glee): the sense that copying itself is most significant as a cultural practice, in ways that override philosophical interest in any specific moment of copying. For

Baudrillard, the general practice of copying holds more fascination than any particular instance, and the artistic practice of "parody makes obedience and transgression equivalent, and this is its most serious crime, since it *cancels out the difference upon which the law is based.*"[24] Parody's ability to critique particular aspects of a culture pales beside the act of copying required for parody, which enacts a more generalized and damaging critique of the cultural concept of the original. Paizs's films display anxiety about the practice of copying, marrying (in their aesthetic forms) an overt practice of celebratory pastiche to a covert angst (expressed in their content).

Paizs's films exemplify pastiche, yet Paizs himself objects to being considered a "pastiche artist." He prefers the term "tribute artist," in the same sense as the musical tribute artists from Steven Penny's first failed beginning to "Crime Wave." Paizs has noted in interviews that "pastiche artist to me sounds like you're trying to hide that you're copying. I'm proud I'm copying and I want people to know I'm copying because I'm doing it in an original way. I'm talking about me through copying films that don't have anything to do with me, that'd be exactly the same whether I existed or not. So I'm copying them but I'm also making them into something they never were."[25] While noting that Paizs's "tribute artistry" is a common technique of postmodern art, and has expected postmodern effects (e.g., the creation of an ironic detachment, alignment with the cultural debris that the copyist admires and enjoys, the sheer enjoyment of repetition itself), we should also note Paizs's claim to a lyrical desire to speak about himself through copying. Perhaps we might see "copying" as a way to recoup lyricism in the wake of the postmodern loss of faith in the possibility of a self that can speak. However, Paizs's alignment with paracinemas – that is, with the "trash" cinemas that exist on the margins of the Hollywood mainstream – seems an ironic undercutting of this possibility, since it can be read as a method of self-marginalization. Paizs's display of fealty to such paracinemas as school safety films and forgotten commercials, through his imitation of their surfaces, sits uneasily alongside his lofty ambitions for *Crime Wave* and the anxiety expressed within both the film and its film-within-a-film regarding Steven Penny's similar (although much more extravagant) desire for success.

Steven Penny's wild dreams of incredible success clash with Paizs's imitation of unsuccessful cultural debris as one example of the ironic deployment of Paizs's appropriations. What is unusual here is not the ironic appropriation itself, but that the irony arises in Paizs's self-mockery of his own attempt to realize success through a pastiche of paracinema forms rather than in the expected parodic critique of the imitated paracinemas (or through the typical "Canadian" approach of crafting "faux-Hollywood" features). Paizs's films and their implied attitudes towards copying remain unusual in the postmodern context, even though copying itself, whether through pastiche or in other practices, has become a hallmark of postmodern art (where it is often coupled, as in parody, with ironic appropriation – the ironic stance of such repetitions often serves as the sole significant variation in postmodern copying). Hutcheon includes a form of copying, "repetition," among the common "tactics used" by postmodern artists to bring ironic "spaces into being" (by which she means liminal spaces).[26] Hutcheon invokes poet Claire Harris to define these liminal spaces as "the space between two worlds" and "a place of paradox," which Hutcheon argues is "also a place of irony."[27] The irony-soaked world of *Crime Wave* is an interesting example of a paradoxical liminal space, insofar as the diegesis in which Steven Penny struggles to write "Crime Wave" is a strange world "between" our world (where we supposedly watch, in *Crime Wave*, Paizs repeat in Penny's story a metafictional tale about the creative process) and Steven Penny's final beginning and ending to "Crime Wave" (where Penny himself repeats Paizs's gesture by producing a metafiction about the creative process). In terms of both content (we see four beginnings and endings to "Crime Wave," Steven repeats his failed attempts to write the film, etc.) and form (through stylistic pastiche), repetition itself is one of the "major strategic rhetorical practices of [Paizs's] postmodern art in general"[28] (here I repeat Hutcheon, with variation) – just as much as the irony to which Hutcheon actually refers in the original quote. Although postmodern in their trappings, Paizs's films take an uneasy stance towards their own irony, which cannot defuse (yet can trouble and complicate) the director's aforementioned personal investment.

The film's own "personal investment" in copying appears not just through its formal technique of pastiche, but in its metafictional structure. Within itself, *Crime Wave* produces multiple beginnings and endings to "Crime Wave." Depending on how you count them (does the first "beginning" of Steven Penny's "Crime Wave," which is also the beginning of John Paizs's *Crime Wave*, get counted twice?), the film contains four or five such beginnings and endings, all of which are to varying degrees copies of one another, with similar structures, plots, and voice-over narration. Baudrillard sutures such postmodern artistic practices to the cultural prevalence of copying and its relation to Freudian repetition, noting that the compulsion to repeat was "what Freud called the death drive ... This process knows neither crisis nor catastrophe: it is hypertelic, in the sense that it has no other end than limitless increase."[29] Although Baudrillard's perspective on copying might seem hysterical, his fundamental observation of the nightmarish qualities of copying has particular resonance, given the frustration felt by Steven Penny, *Crime Wave*'s author-protagonist, at his failure to produce "Crime Wave" – and given the dark undercurrents that run beneath Penny's fantasies and Paizs's film. The above-noted enjoyment of repetition that results in and through pastiche should, then, be couched in this Freudian observation that repetition is not aligned with pleasure so much as with a drive that transcends pleasure, repeating destructively in mad attempts at "limitless increase." This is certainly apparent in Steven Penny's "final" ending to "Crime Wave," a fantasy wherein he imagines greater and greater successes for his metafictional double, all of which collapse after he fails to satisfy "Steven." Such a death drive (to repeat the words of Žižek), "finds satisfaction in endlessly repeating the same failed gesture."[30] Steven Penny's rewriting of the beginnings and endings to "Crime Wave" (necessary due to his failure to write middles, and thus "Crime Wave"), and his discontent even within the success-fantasy of his "final" ending to "Crime Wave," both attest to a strange sort of "satisfaction" in repetition. Although his repetitions do not satisfy him in the sense that he does not succeed through repeating, the act of repetition satisfies his desire to imagine success in an illusory future where some final act of writing might produce a satisfactory film.

However, the narrative logic of *Crime Wave* compels Steven Penny to actually produce this "final" ending, to realize his fantasy. The necessary stoppage of what could otherwise be an endless series of repetitions underscores the absence of the impossible object that is the film "Crime Wave" itself, prompting Penny to (as his "final" repetition) repeat himself within the script by turning "Crime Wave" into a metafiction (thus turning from the "color crime" genre in a manner that underlines his failure). Here the distinction between Paizs's *Crime Wave* and Penny's "Crime Wave" must be insisted upon. While Steven Penny fantasizes the possession/creation of "Crime Wave" in a way that reveals its status as an impossible object, Paizs's film *Crime Wave* does not stand as the fulfilment of this fantasy. In other words, the equation of the two films is not sustainable at this point, despite its suggestion within the narrative and the fact that they have both become metafictions through Steven Penny's final screenwriting act. Instead, a gap exists between *Crime Wave* and "Crime Wave," and Paizs's film obsessively worries that gap. This is why the plot of Steven's "final" ending repeatedly insists on both the success of "Steven Penny" and his lack of satisfaction in realizing this success. The realization of Steven's fantasy is also its dissolution, so that his successful production of a "final" ending to "Crime Wave" stands as an ironic insistence on his failure to produce "Crime Wave." By making this failure the subject of *Crime Wave*, John Paizs has crafted a far different film from the typical Hollywood movie it nonetheless purports to copy. *Crime Wave* insists upon the gap that "Crime Wave" tries to fill, rather than the usual operation of Hollywood film, whereby the narrative "fills in" such gaps by dramatizing the fulfilment of various fantasies for the characters, in a manner that supports or enacts the audience's own fantasy fulfilment.

The Failure of Fantasy

As Hillel Schwartz displays, in *The Culture of the Copy*,[31] copying as an aesthetic practice persists throughout and across cultures and periods, and is fundamental to the notion of culture itself (for cultures to exist, ideologies must repeat; as Boon notes, "even the ideology of individuality and/or uniqueness is mass-produced.")[32] Appropriately, copying is not just the subject of cultural theories like Schwartz's, but often part and parcel of theoretical practice itself, which repeats and modifies already existing ideas while literally reproducing the words of previous authors through citation. The writings of Slavoj Žižek, despite his antipathy for postmodernism, stand as exemplary of this postmodern literary practice of pastiche: Žižek will often copy the words of other writers, with variations he then notes and makes the subject of his discussion, and will even copy his own insights, structures of argument, and written passages from book to book. Moreover, Žižek presents himself not just as a student of both Lacan and Hegel, but also to some degree as a repetition of both. Žižek's "return to Lacan" extends Lacan's theory through a Hegelian lens (or vice versa), in the same way that Lacan's "return to Freud" presented itself as a project that discovered, already latent within Freud's work, various ideas of which Freud himself was unaware (in a sense, repeating Freud's psychoanalytic procedure to interpret not dreams but *The Interpretation of Dreams*). Lacan presents himself as reproducing Freud's work in a form supposedly more faithful to Freud than Freud himself could manage, before developments in other disciplines, and Žižek repeats this gesture by reproducing Lacan's theories in a Hegelian light that Žižek proposes was already latent in Lacan's work. Psychoanalytic theory, then, often presents itself as "continuing the master's work" while extending and overwriting the original: copying or "doubling" is an integral concept both within the theory and in its historical development. Thus Žižek appears as a "tribute artist" who "covers" Lacan himself a "tribute artist" who repeats Freud – who used to comment that all of his "original" insights were to be found, already, in Nietzsche – who, in a similar fashion, cited the influence of Dostoevsky. There are many political and rhetorical reasons for these kinds of gestures – including a diplomatic borrowing of authority under the cover of a concomitant ceding of authority, and as a modelling of the psychoanalytic method of "discovering" repression encoded in/created by the symptom – but such gestures are also, as Paizs's work makes clear, artistic and aesthetic choices. As well, Hutcheon would surely note, they are ironic gestures (in the psychoanalytic example, an ironic insistence on servitude designed to secure and display mastery).

By the time that *Crime Wave*'s copying produces the final beginning and ending to "Crime Wave," Paizs's metafiction has become explicitly self-reflexive, a *mise en abyme* structure. Within this abyss, the fantasy that sustains the film (Steven Penny's dreamed creation of "Crime Wave") is revealed as an ironic dream, since Steven encodes within his fantasy its impossibility and inevitable failure. For Žižek, one of the fundamental qualities of fantasy is that "fantasy is the primordial form of narrative, which serves to occult some original deadlock,"[33] and we can connect Steven's continual attempts at narrative creation to his attempts to construct and enjoy his fantasy of success (which, in his mind if not in practical fact, amounts to the same thing as creating an acceptable script for "Crime Wave"). The narrative drive throughout *Crime Wave*, especially in Steven Penny's final ending to "Crime Wave," comes close to operating like a psychoanalytic drive (in its satisfaction through repetition, as noted above). Quite apart from Penny's conscious desire, which is to complete rather than repeat the action of writing "Crime Wave," stands his unconscious knowledge of its impossibility. This repressed unconscious knowledge finds expression in his final scripted ending, where Penny writes himself into "Crime Wave," in a fantasy of wild success. Fantasy, of course, is another abyss, especially in Žižek's view that fantasy stands as the necessary support of a subject's sense of reality, which stems from trauma and whose actual realization, therefore, is doubly traumatic.

"Doubly traumatic" also in the sense of doubling (copying) trauma, for the realization of this final fantasy, the creation of his final beginning and ending, finds Steven inscribing within the script (and thus within Paizs's film) a series of disappointments, failure where we expect triumph. At the same time, since Steven writes himself into the script, he produces his own double/doppelgänger, copying himself. Hillel Schwartz connects the practice of copying to Freudian concepts of subject formation (concepts that have been revitalized more recently by Žižek to explain the role of ideology in cultural formations). As Schwartz notes:

> Freud was drawn to the *unheimlich* or unsettling or uncanny, whose definition he borrowed [copied] from the philosopher Friedrich Schelling: that which "ought to have remained secret and hidden but has come to light." Psychoanalysis itself could seem uncanny, for it brought what was repressed into the open. Yet, "When all is said and done," wrote Freud, "the quality of uncanniness can only come from the fact of the 'double'

> being a creation dating back to a very early mental stage, long since surmounted – a stage, incidentally, at which it wore a more friendly aspect. The 'double' has become a thing of terror, just as, after the collapse of their religions, the gods turned into demons."[34]

Schwartz, through Freud, thus suggests a form of copying that produces change: in Freud's formulation, the gods become demons through doubling, gaining power via repression and subsequent return (in uncanny repetition). In addition, the altered context of their reappearance intensifies the terror of their repetition. A world that disavows these gods, in which their renewed presence constitutes a disturbance, lends them uncanny power. Paizs's filmmaking practice of pastiche similarly reproduces the "dead" forms of bygone paracinemas, to transform "trash" into art, but Paizs's "tribute artistry" is not in line with Duchampian or Warholian reproduction, since Paizs uses these paracinemas as models rather than as readymades. Paizs's copying is also more anxious, more Freudian, than the joyful reproduction of "trash" in a John Waters film, especially given Paizs's mixture of celebration and unease when reproducing B-movie tropes of violence.

Although Steven Penny attempts to fashion an acceptable, sustainable fantasy by producing his uncanny double in the final beginning and ending to "Crime Wave," the (doubly) fictional "Steven Penny" remains dissatisfied, aware of the impossible nature of his desire to create "Crime Wave." The fantasy fails even as it is elaborated: the film-within-a-film's protagonist-"Steven" grows more glum as author-Penny grants him every possible success. Within the final ending of "Crime Wave," the last words of "Steven Penny" ("I real ly did mean to be good") – doubly authored by Steven (writer of the scenario) and "Steven" (typewriter within the scene) – apologize for having failed, even as the same narrator who appeared throughout the other beginnings and endings returns to trumpet his triumph. The self-awareness that the fictionalized

"Steven" shows in this final ending to "Crime Wave" appears nowhere in its first beginning and ending, and this necessitates the production of his second beginning and ending, and so on, until Penny "completes" his script by authoring its "final" beginning and ending, where all of his fantasies come to life (except, it must be noted, his impossible desire to create "Crime Wave"). Of course, as Baudrillard writes (in a sentence that might have been authored by Žižek), "nothing is worse than to utter a wish and to have it literally fulfilled; nothing is worse than to be rewarded on the exact level of one's demand."[35]

The reason, as Žižek notes, is that the human condition (insofar as this phrase might still mean anything, after postmodernism's dismantling of universals) is to be a "decentred subject" (this insight is the basis for Žižek's post-postmodern attempt to revitalize the category of the subject, which had been dismantled in postmodernism). By this Žižek means a subject "deprived of even my most intimate 'subjective' experience, the way things 'really seem to me,' that of the fundamental fantasy that constitutes and guarantees the core of my being, since I can never consciously experience it and assume it" without destabilizing and destroying that selfsame subjectivity.[36] It is for this reason that "the core of our fantasy is unbearable to us."[37] However, Penny *does* "experience and assume" his fantasy: he writes "Crime Wave" – or at least, he *seems* to ... in fact, in its writing he discovers not only that he will never write "Crime Wave" but also that this achievement would mean nothing. Insofar as he has managed to "consciously experience it and assume it," Penny's fantasy fails and results in the dismantling of reality (in the film, a narrative breakdown or collapse between metafictional levels, evident throughout the course of *Crime Wave*) and subjective destitution.

Steven Penny, this "quiet man" who never speaks, is barely a character to begin with; furthermore, his "quiet man" identity was produced by Paizs in earlier short films and moved from film to film until it was copied again in *Crime Wave*. Steven Penny not only produces his own uncanny double in the course of *Crime Wave*'s metafiction, but also himself is the uncanny double of characters from Paizs's earlier 1980s films (Billy Botski and Nick – these characters and their films are discussed more fully in chapter 2). Paizs's copying does not stop and start with the paracinema models for his pastiche: copying is an essential part of Paizs's own oeuvre, and the copying of characteristics across characters suggests a postmodern lack of faith in identity itself. Paizs's "quiet man" has no depth, but is a collection of surfaces, a body and face presented as blankly as possible, marked as anachronistic and abnormal within both the narrative space and the cinematic space by his lack of voice. No narrative explanation, other than the quirk of being "quiet," ever explains this throwback to an age before sync sound. The copying (with its variations) of the quiet man identity from film to film accords with a postmodern perspective. There is no interiority or "depth" beyond the filmic surface, no impossible-to-copy essence or individualism to these "quiet man" characters. This postmodern insistence on identity as a set of copy-able surfaces is distinct from, but related to, the post-structuralist conception of Lacanian subjectivity as a "lack" with ontological status. Whereas the postmodern subject is illusory (without essence), the Lacanian subject exists as an absence (a "lack") with illusory consistency due to the circulation of its surfaces around a fantasy of possible wholeness (a fantasy of essence). The transportable figure of Paizs's "quiet man" operates to link these conceptions of identity. While the "quiet man" character remains a set of signifiers that signify nothing but draw attention to themselves, the manner in which the "quiet man" appears (varies) when copied to *Crime Wave* involves its (Steven Penny's) attempt to find purchase in reality by producing the fantasy of writing "Crime Wave" to guarantee or give meaning to this subject (an effort doomed to failure, since the fantasy depends on the possibility that Steven Penny will write "Crime Wave" but the film's narrative logic both requires and reveals its impossibility).

Steven Penny's inability to grasp what he desires (even in the moment that he seems to produce his final script and grant himself further wishes within that script) also speaks to a fundamental quality of desire, in Žižek's sense that "fantasy" fills in perspectival gaps to prevent any contact with "the real," which is always disappointing and traumatic. Steven's last words, typewritten so that a gap in the word "really" separates out the word "real," seems to acknowledge the always imperfect nature of fantasy, which seeks to fulfil a desire but instead produces desire (in doomed attempts to fill in or close its gaps). Steven's fantasy fulfilments just spawn further, greater wishes, whose fulfilments spawn more, until they collapse under their own impossibility. Prior to this final failure of Steven's fantasy, this fantasy does serve to structure the film, which is the story of how Steven attempts to write "Crime Wave," and which culminates in a "happy ending" where he does write "Crime Wave," even though the "final" ending's metafictional structure and dark, ironic content together undercut its colourful surface. As Žižek notes, "fantasy is on the side of reality ... it sustains the subject's 'sense of reality': when the phantasmatic frame disintegrates, the subject undergoes a 'loss of reality' and starts to perceive reality as an 'irreal' nightmarish universe with no firm ontological foundation."[38] Similarly, as Steven moves closer to his fantasy of writing "Crime Wave" and therefore, ironically, comes closer to the realization of its impossibility, both the character and the filmed world in which he exists lose this "sense of reality": the filmed world becomes increasingly artificial (with unnatural lighting, unbelievable plot developments, and backgrounds painted on glass).

Crime Wave was always, because of its pastiche aesthetic, artificial and non-realistic, so even before becoming explicit as the film's tone darkens, this "nightmarish universe" persists as an undercurrent within the film. Paizs symbolizes this dark undercurrent in the cinematic image of the black/blank screen between filmic frames, always present but not consciously accessible due to the phenomenon of persistence of vision, a phenomenon that Kim and Steven explain to the viewer in a further postmodern flourish. Unlike the conventional Hollywood film, which offers to fulfil fantasies through escapism, *Crime Wave* promises fulfilment and then delivers its lie. By presenting itself, through pastiche and metafiction, as a copy of a film ("Crime Wave") that never had and never could have a real existence, *Crime Wave* draws attention throughout to the black screen underlying its surface flashes, insisting on the eternal emptiness of the gap it claims to fill.

As well, the pseudo-documentary style and structure of *Crime Wave* both masks and reveals the film's lack of a "firm ontological foundation." Kim's narration throughout the movie attempts to gloss over and fill in gaps in its fractured narrative, an operation that has the ironic effect of emphasizing these gaps. However, *Crime Wave* still, to some degree, "wants nothing more than to be a 'color crime movie,'"[39] despite all of its play with conventions. The film thus exhibits a particularly Canadian schizophrenia. *Crime Wave* wants to be a sensational, American crime movie, replete with pop-culture Americana such as a go-getting Elvis impersonator. Yet *Crime Wave* takes the form of an awkward documentary, some National Film Board production about an obscure Canadian artist.

The Canadian Dream

Since *Crime Wave* seems to stand as a postmodern film with a psychoanalytic structure, whose narrative effectively presents an artist traversing his fantasy and thus arriving at subjective destitution – a state that allows for the postmodern traverse of Paizs's "quiet man" figure from film to film – *Crime Wave* can best be understood through a theoretical pastiche that blends otherwise incommensurate philosophical positions. Postmodern theorists such as Hutcheon root Canadian identity in irony and thus typify the Canadian as a particularly postmodern subject, whereas psychoanalytic theorists like Žižek ground cultural identity in a shared experience of traumatic lack and, therefore, fantasy. *Crime Wave* bridges this seeming gap: Steven Penny's failure to produce "Crime Wave," the color crime movie that will secure his artistic legacy, is on one level a failure to be American, and it is this particularly ironic desire that we might read almost allegorically as an impossible desire in Žižek's sense.

It would be going too far to suggest that the Canadian, reclined on the analyst's couch, wants to be an American in his secret heart. Although the multiculturalist pose often doubles for or attempts to replace a sense of national identity, the concept of a cultural mosaic renders suspect the notion that Canadians could possibly "share" any sort of cultural experience. If, like Žižek, we limit discussion to ideological "realities," and speak of the illusory phantasm of the "Canadian" that haunts cultural discourse, then the argument carries more weight. Certainly, in the sociopolitical context of the 1980s, with the then-seeming invincibility of the U.S.'s imperial might, this impossible/ironic desire to Americanize seems more plausible. At the same time, Canadian resistance to Americanization has historically centred around anxieties concerning threats to or potential for some national identity. Regardless of reality, in the public imagination and in the subtextual heart of Paizs's film, the impression of Canadian inferiority, the "little brother" complex, remains rooted – in the period if not in perpetuity.

The complex ontological status of *Crime Wave*'s narrative world, its metafictional qualities, again become salient. In line with Brian McHale's notion of postmodern art as "dominated by ontological issues,"[40] *Crime Wave* suggests an ontological unease concerning Canadian identity and culture – anxiety about the degree to which they might exist after the onslaught of American culture or even *because of* this onslaught. Steven Penny's fantasy of crafting the greatest color crime movie ever made, and his attempts to do so, reveal a desire to be assimilated into America even while retaining some distance from it – thus displaying both fascination and abhorrence in the face of its culture of violence. This attraction and repulsion is inherent in Paizs's status as a "tribute artist" employing an aesthetic of copying. *Crime Wave* self-consciously points to, and appears conflicted about, this artistic approach, connecting practices of imitation with acts of violence to suggest a fundamental ambivalence about its own appropriation of the trappings of American cinema. The narrative collapse between ontological levels appears coextensive with Steven Penny's travel into the United States (from Canadian soil to American dream, where the film's already tenuous "reality" loses its meaning and ground). *Crime Wave* thereby displays fundamental anxieties about its existence as a Canadian cultural product that apes American cultural products, mirrored in its diegetic indeterminacy.

Through the metafictional inscription of its final beginning and ending, "Crime Wave" becomes at once a realization of Steven Penny's desires (the actual manifestation of his dreamed film, his out-Hollywooding of Hollywood) and an admission of failure, of the impossibility of realizing this selfsame dream (due to Penny being, like Paizs, a Canadian artist producing independent cinema on the prairies). Steven's final beginning and ending to "Crime Wave" self-reflexively posit the imagined film-within-a-film as a fantasy space that ruptures to expose its own failure to produce an inhabitable reality. By extension, *Crime Wave* suggests the inability of Canadian culture, and the Canadian cinema, to exist in any stable, definable form. Ironically, the film presents this indeterminacy as a model for a state of productive anxiety that might move beyond the deadlock of either repeating or resisting American culture.

Pevere writes that "while remaining principally and effectively a comedy, *Crime Wave* ponders such pertinent but unlikely laugh-fodder as the relationship between culture and social behaviour; Canadian cultural Ameriphilia and its schizoid effects, creative stagnation, and the perpetually self-replenishing nature of popular culture."[41] While remaining principally and effectively an argument concerning *Crime Wave*'s status as a postmodern artefact, my analysis ponders such pertinent critical fodder as *Crime Wave*'s complex metafictional structure, pastiche aesthetics, pervasive undercurrent of violence, and ironic insistence on failure as the manifest destiny of the Canadian artist. Owing to such qualities, *Crime Wave* stands as an exemplary work of postmodern art. At the same time, it expresses deep anxieties about this postmodern state of being. As a result, John Paizs's *Crime Wave* seems neither dated nor limited by its alignment with artistic and philosophic modes of critique popular during the period of its production – another reason why the work of a more recent (and non-postmodern) theorist like Žižek seems necessary to its critical discussion. Against all odds, and despite its neglect, John Paizs's *Crime Wave* therefore continues to have relevance in an age when postmodernism has lost its radicality, to be greeted with either a doe-eyed acceptance or a steely-gazed scepticism. Although postmodern in its trappings, *Crime Wave* suggests the limitations of postmodernism as an "ism" through a recognition of the mutable nature of reality that is deeply anxious rather than blithely celebratory. At the same time, *Crime Wave* adopts a radical stance through this state of anxiety, rather than falling back on the expected conservative position. Pevere notes that, through *Crime Wave*, Paizs examines "Canadian cultural Ameriphilia and its schizoid effects."[42] In that examination, *Crime Wave* goes beyond the standard Canadian critique of presenting American cultural influence as lamentable, inescapable doom.

Will Straw writes of "a commonplace of English-Canadian cultural criticism that many of our most revealing works are characterized by the ironic appropriation of those cultures which dominate us," and that "this clearly helps illuminate the films of John Paizs, so many of which engage with the paracinemas of U.S. industrial films and 1950s cartoons."[43] *Crime Wave*'s engagement with such "paracinemas" through pastiche does constitute an "ironic appropriation" of American cultural debris, but *Crime Wave* also provides oblique commentary on the perpetual anxieties that surround Canadian notions of a national cinema itself. Andrew Higson writes that "the concept of a national cinema has almost invariably been mobilized as a strategy of cultural (and economic) resistance: a means of asserting national autonomy in the face of (usually) Hollywood's international domination."[44] *Crime Wave*'s nationalist project, insofar as the phrase seems sensible, differs in scope. In its content, Paizs's film appears to mount a comedic critique of "Hollywood international domination" and American cultural hegemony, but its form is one of affectionate (yet anxious) imitation. Rather than copying to impress, or making a point of abandoning our attempts to be like our "big brother" to the south – either pose being to define ourselves through this relation – the film suggests that we abandon the attempt to abandon this attempt, and copy with impunity what we will. *Crime Wave* thus stands, in its contemporaneous context and even today, as a meditation on the possibility of a nationalist cinema, a warning against a nationalist cinema, and a model for a nationalist cinema in a U.S.-dominated industry.

2

Beginnings and Endings

John Paizs was born in Winnipeg in 1957, and his childhood influences were typically Canadian, in the sense that they were American. To be Canadian at the time meant, for Geoff Pevere, to "live in one place [when] what you enjoyed all came from somewhere else."[1] Paizs's 1980s work – his most significant – bears the clear influence of American comic books, sitcoms, educational films, movie trailers, commercials, B-movie genre thrillers, and cartoons (often this influence appears through direct imitation of these models). Paizs's artistic ambitions have always been tied to such fare: "Originally, I wanted to be a comic book artist, and I started making my own superhero and horror comics in junior high school. At this same time, I also started experimenting with film, with my dad's 8mm camera. But I didn't decide to focus on film until my first year of university, when I bought a Bolex camera, a few lights and a tripod, and started making films in 16mm."[2]

Around 1970, Paizs set down his father's 8mm camera and began working with his own Super 8mm camera. His first Super 8mm film was called *Beyond the Universe* (1974). From 1975 to 1976, Paizs worked at Kenn Perkins Animation Ltd. as an animator. One of Paizs's colleagues at Kenn Perkins, Cordell Barker, later directed a number of animated films, including *The Cat Came Back* (1988) and *Strange Invaders* (2001), which both earned Academy Award nominations. At Kenn Perkins, Paizs worked on

John Paizs with light meter on the set of *Crime Wave*. Courtesy of John Paizs, from the director's personal collection.

a host of projects ranging from respected fare like cartoons for *Sesame Street* to tacky K-Tel International television commercials, "hawking such projects as the *Kooky Kountry* record album . . . and *Goofy Greats*"[3] (the latter includes the novelty hit song "The Purple People Eater"). Paizs pays homage to such disposable fare in his films, most obviously through the "House of Tomorrow" segment of *Springtime in Greenland*, where characters become giddy over modern conveniences like lawn sprinklers. Although "a dream job"[4] for Paizs at the time, he had always planned to, and did, leave Kenn Perkins to travel Europe before returning to Winnipeg to enrol in the University of Manitoba's School of Art. Paizs attended from 1977 to 1980, majoring in photography while making his own animated films.

Paizs's animated films begin with *The Nine to Five Crack* (1977), which was shot in Super 8mm during 1974 and 1975, while Paizs was still in high school.[5] In 1977, Paizs reshot the film in 16mm and added sound.[6] Paizs worked on *The Dreamer* (1978) from 1976 to 1978,[7] which Gene Walz describes as "an imitation Disney movie with full-blown backgrounds, symphonic music, and a cute elephant chased through a castle by a devilish monster."[8] Paizs also completed *Hoedown* (1977), which "was drawn directly onto blank 16mm with coloured felt markers, a technique Norman McLaren had used."[9] *The Dreamer* won Paizs an award from the British Film Institute for Outstanding Film of the Year at the 1978 London Film Festival.[10] Yet Paizs abandoned animation despite this success due to its work-intensive processes, thinking he'd see a higher return on his efforts from live-action filmmaking.

Paizs began his live-action career with the 16mm *The Warrior* (1978), "with images of a drunk in an alley visited by allegorical figures – Religion, Business, Death – accompanied by the music of Emerson, Lake, and Palmer,"[11] and followed this with a science fiction comedy called *Ed Zorax of the Future City* (1979). However, it was with *The Obsession of Billy Botski* that Paizs began to change the face of Winnipeg cinema.

The Obsession of Billy Botski (1980)

Obsession was the film that spurred Guy Maddin to direct his debut film, *The Dead Father:* "I was just bowled over by the fact that this was a film made in Canada, in Winnipeg ... It was exactly half an hour long and I knew ... I'd make a half-hour movie."[12] For many others, as noted by Patrick Lowe, *Obsession* was and remains "a touchstone film for the [Winnipeg Film Group's] patent style of deadpan, garish comedy."[13] *Obsession* is also a seminal film in Paizs's own oeuvre, since the character of Billy Botski marks the advent of the "quiet man" character that reappears in all of Paizs's major films. This "quiet man" character materializes in three incarnations: first as Billy Botski, then as Nick in the short film trilogy *The Three Worlds of Nick,* and finally as Steven Penny in *Crime Wave.* None of these characters speaks on-screen: Billy's voice-over narrates a film in which he does not otherwise speak, Nick never speaks, and third-party narrators report Steven's speech. Paizs himself performs as each figure, without affectation or costume to distinguish one from the other. Paizs's recurrent "quiet man" is a social misfit and an anachronism: in the words of Paizs, "a Buster Keaton-like character in the sound era."[14] Always held from the audience at an ironic distance, this "quiet man" is often comic and sometimes endearing, but never wholly sympathetic.

Billy stands as the least sympathetic, and creepiest, of Paizs's creations. Obsessed with "Connie," a pop-culture Playboy Bunny ideal of the (as Billy puts it) "mythical virgin slut," Billy searches for her in reality. Billy's fantasies come to life and die on the same strange night. After an awkward flirtation at a party, Billy meets with "Connie" at a seedy motel. In the midst of their embrace, her body goes limp. Billy hangs on to Connie's corpse, hopeful of a resurrection, although he soon dumps her into the river. Robert L. Cagle notes that "Billy's existence is an unstable mix of fantasy and reality organized by images and surfaces,"[15] most obviously those "images [of various "Connies"] from the magazines and album covers that fill Billy's home,"[16] some of them pornographic. Billy's obsessive interest in "Connies" is mirrored in the film's own aesthetic interest in the duplication of iconic American imagery (even the name "Connie" suggests the word "icon"). Thus, as Cagle writes, *Obsession* "is a fascinating assemblage of intertextual references – of surfaces – that alternately conceals and reveals its origins in the mythology of American popular culture."[17] This manner of aping the imagery and style of American popular culture, in a way that both "conceals" its (often obscure) origins and "reveals" its indebtedness to and affection for the same, is distinctive of Paizs's 1980s films and their postmodern pastiche.

Obsession at first seems to encourage us to read Billy's dumping of Connie's dead body metaphorically, as maturation – thus suggesting that obsessive pursuit of media-constructed fantasies can, and should, be curtailed. After a disappointing encounter with a real woman, Billy grows up and moves on from his unrealistic fantasies. However, corpse disposal as a method of "moving on" has obvious negative connotations that frustrate the desire to read this scene metaphorically. Moreover, as Cagle points out, Connie is less of a "real woman" than "the sum total of a system of simulations, a person 'passing' as a woman."[18] The disturbing nature of the plot's development, with its half-suggestion of necrophilia, undercuts any reading of progressive maturation through the (here literal) disposal of Billy's fantasies. An unsettling film results, one that dramatizes its own anxiety about such interplay of "images and surfaces."

Billy's fetishistic interest in surfaces finds itself mirrored in the cinematic attention of the camera, suggesting the complicity of both filmmaker and filmgoer through this prurient attention. Laura Mulvey sees this same dynamic as a troubling and misogynistic quality of conventional narrative cinema in general, one revealed and explored in certain films of Alfred Hitchcock, where "the spectator ... finds himself exposed as complicit, caught in the moral ambiguity of looking."[19] Whatever the weaknesses of Mulvey's theory (for instance, like the psychoanalytic theory upon which Mulvey builds, it offers little legroom for lesbian desire), it does account for certain ways that "the presence of woman is an indispensable element of spectacle in normal narrative film"[20] and how "the cinema satisfies a primordial wish for pleasurable looking."[21] *Obsession* presents Billy's desires as just such a cinematic wish, with "Connie" both formed from and collapsing beneath the weight of Billy's fantasies, which cannot be divorced from media representations of popular culture and cinema history.

Springtime in Greenland (1981)

In Paizs's next film, *Springtime in Greenland,* he again plays the "quiet man," now named Nick after Hemingway's alter ego in his coming-of-age stories. Nick appears in three films, later screened together as the feature-length program *The Three Worlds of Nick.* Paizs has stated that "[I] always meant [these films] to be a trilogy – a feature, actually, that I could finance and make in manageable stages."[22] Each film announces itself as part of a larger series, through opening title cards: in order, they read "The First World ... Nick at home" (*Springtime in Greenland*), "The Second World ... Nick learns something" (*Oak, Ivy, and Other Dead Elms*) and "The Third World ... Nick finds love" (*The International Style*). *The Three Worlds of Nick* might be considered Paizs's avant-garde feature film debut, and deserves rediscovery as much as *Crime Wave.*

Beginning similarly in a documentary style, *Springtime* first differs from *Obsession* through its third-party narrator (and his bizarre intonations). Unlike Billy Botski, *Springtime*'s narrator is not also a character in the film, and he has no special access to Nick's interior world of thoughts and feelings. This development separates the viewer from the silent Paizs character, to hide Nick's inner life.

The creation and refinement of the "quiet man" character, who appears in various incarnations across Paizs's five 1980s films, marks these works as particularly postmodern through the figure's ironic anachronism, intertextual transformations, and destabilizing presence. At first, playing the protagonist of his own films was a matter of necessity for Paizs: because he could only shoot erratically due to his schedule and finances, Paizs cast himself as a lead actor who could be available whenever he was, at a moment's notice, without pay. The character's silence developed pragmatically: because Paizs didn't like his voice and didn't think he could act, he decided on silence and blank expressions.[23] Although initially a matter of convenience, Paizs's manner of building films around his own on-screen appearance, as a figure who is marked and isolated by silence and blankness, has distinctive postmodern qualities. In McHale's terms, "the fictional world now acquires a visible marker" of its created status due "to the artist's paradoxical self-representation."[24] Although in the films Paizs presents himself as "Nick" and not as an author-figure (a distinction that collapses in *Crime Wave*), by appearing as "Nick" in a mannered way that marks his appearance as artificial and performative, Paizs draws attention to his performance *as* performance. Thus, as with the self-presence of the author, "the artwork itself comes to be presented *as* an artwork."[25] However, Paizs always *seeming* to be Paizs yet never *claiming* to be Paizs allows the film's narrative world to retain a certain stability despite the auteur's destabilizing presence.

The "quiet man" figure becomes all the more strange through his transmutations from film to film (all differing in their styles and genres) and name to name (from Billy to Nick to Steven). Thus Paizs's 1980s films allude to one another as they signal their own artifice. Discrete and self-contained, while also parts of a larger set, Paizs's "quiet man" films draw attention to Paizs's own status as author of their filmed worlds. Paizs has incorporated, alongside elements from popular culture, elements from his own productions – even his own self (a gesture that suggests the unnatural nature of the postmodern self). Yet unlike most similar postmodern appearances of the author, Paizs does not draw the audience close in a demystification of narrative processes (something Paizs later does in *Crime Wave*); rather, he uses his own body to further inscribe emotional distance.

Nick, as acted blankly by Paizs, is unknowable. When narration appears, or other characters speak directly to (or of) Nick, it does not serve to enlighten us. Others have no insight into Nick's character, and the viewer's position lacks privileged access to Nick's private moments. The resulting figure serves as a screen upon which the audience can project Nick's imagined personality (like the fantasy space of the cinema screen itself), yet they cannot identify with Nick since Paizs refuses to affirm any such projections. Nick (like, later, Steven Penny) seems fated, therefore, to become a social outcast. This misfit position is supported in formal terms through the anachronism of the "quiet man" character.

Nick's underdog or outsider status does not make him lovable by default. He appears self-conscious, even haughty, and his victimization seems at once deplorable and appropriate. Nick's antagonist in *Springtime* is Corny Blower, who, Cagle observes, "like 'Connie' in *Obsession*, is a collection of gender stereotypes."[26] Nick is cheated and teased by the brutish Corny in a backyard diving competition, and instigates a fistfight. We may not be surprised at Nick's violent lashing out, and may even sympathize with him in this moment. But afterwards, when all have gone home, Nick remains: crouched over the pool in the night, pulling black water onto his face like something inhuman (hardly a figure with whom we're asked to identify), some primal creature at the edge of the ocean from which it just crawled.

Springtime is notable for its unusual structure, which falls into five rough acts. The first "act" is styled like a documentary about the bucolic suburb of Greenland, with Nick and his family introduced by a drawling, erratic narrator. In what we might consider a second act, the documentary and its narration give way to a disturbing night scene styled more cinematically. Nick awakens during a thunderstorm and steps out on the front lawn. Inscrutable in his motivations, Nick stares at his family's home from the outside (perhaps to confirm his outsider status). As if unable to bear Nick's scrutiny, the film escapes to a third act, this time a bizarre commercial sequence during which a new narrator trumpets the technological wonders offered by "The House of Tomorrow." *Springtime* returns, in its fourth act, to the pool party and its masculine competition between Corny and Nick. After the fallout of their brief brawl, a fifth act provides a coda, as our first drawling narrator returns to celebrate Greenland's spring parade (which Nick skips, although his dog settles in for the spectacle).

Springtime's structural symmetry confirms the central position of the "House of Tomorrow" segment and its consumerist ideology. At the film's heart lies the commercial "The House of Tomorrow," nestled between two cinematic sequences about Nick; in turn, all of this is framed between two documentary sequences about Greenland. Cagle notes that this commercial "segment is an exact replica, played with deadpan earnestness, of countless promotional films aimed at housewives and newlyweds. The message of these short subjects was as unvarying as it was clear: domestic bliss can be attained only through conspicuous consumption."[27] Thus, in copying the style of commercials and promotional films, Paizs also reproduces their ideological assumptions. When decontextualized in this way, these assumptions are laid bare and their absurdity is plain to see: an implicit critique develops through ironic appropriation of these surfaces. Yet Paizs seems, at the same time, to love these surfaces. He copies their style in imitation rather than copying the original texts whole – for example, instead of stitching together already existing clips in the manner of films like *The Atomic Cafe* (1982). Copying in *The Atomic Cafe* manifests itself in ironic montages of American propaganda films, assembled to present a nuclear attack on the United States: the implication is that the logical terminus of militaristic foreign policy is boomerang-style annihilation. Paizs's approach, although it still fuses irony with critical undertones, is less biting, less directly political, and more ambivalent.

"The House of Tomorrow" segment features a much more vibrant narrator than the first segment of *Springtime*, and this second narrator (Douglas Syms) will later return to lead us through the beginnings and endings of Steven Penny's failed screenplay in *Crime Wave*. Neil Lawrie, the actor playing the patriarch of this "House of Tomorrow," will also return in *Crime Wave* as the deranged serial sex murderer Dr C. Jolly. Connecting the two figures, or even considering them identical, seems a tempting although radical reading, given Paizs's other metafictional games and the pathology that informs this commercial segment. The viewer cannot possibly be as excited about "The House of Tomorrow" as the characters in the film, who orgasmically respond to banalities like thermostats, electric lights, toasters, and lawn sprinklers. Lawrie's appearance in *Springtime* as proud patriarch of a consumerist paradise, and his reappearance in *Crime Wave* as the murderous Dr Jolly, suggest a natural evolution from one figure into the other, although little in *Crime Wave* connects Dr Jolly to consumer culture. However, Jolly does lure his victims by claiming to be a Hollywood script doctor, and thus he serves as a stitch that sutures *Crime Wave*'s thematic obsession with violence to the capitalist ambitions and colonial reach of the American cinema.

Without explanation or context, "The House of Tomorrow" segment prefigures (in its tone of deadpan irony) the sketch comedy of *The Kids in the Hall*, a show for which Paizs later directed. This "House of Tomorrow" commercial, not unlike the angular plots of sketch comedy, seems like a digression more than a progression, in that it has no explicit connection to Greenland or Nick. However, as Pevere has written, the commercial segment "effectively provides a kind of pop-ideology context for the absurd middle-class melodrama being played out around the sun-baked backyard barbecue ... A dialectic of sorts is established between the expository mock-documentary passages and the poolside showdown that effectively suggests a cause-and-effect relationship between them: mindless media messages make for mindless behaviour."[28]

Pevere's insight is apt but fails to account for the structural symmetry of *Springtime* and its *two* levels of mock-documentary (the erratic narration concerning suburban Greenland, which opens and closes the film, and the earnest narration concerning "The House of Tomorrow"). It is not simply that media messages have distorted reality: reality itself is coextensive with media fantasy. In the world of *Springtime*, it is senseless to seek cause-and-effect relationships between suburban reality and commercial fantasy. One does not produce the other, to then feed back in a series of dialectic exchanges. In his analysis, Pevere argues that only in the later Nick films does this "distinction between the world of the drama and the world perpetrated in and by the media"[29] collapse. However, as the pseudo-documentary frame of the opening and closing segments makes clear, this distinction has already suffered a postmodern collapse in *Springtime*, where suburban "reality" is itself a commercial fantasy. The framing narration attempts to sell us on the virtues of Springtime in Greenland, as if *Springtime* as a whole were a promotional film for suburban development. That is, a commercial housing another commercial, since within just such a middle-class milieu we find "The House of Tomorrow" (although most of the story's action takes place outdoors, around the backyard pool, and no significant attempt is made to suggest that Nick's house is a technological wonder).

The only person who isn't convinced of these values, who isn't buying (at least, not yet), is Nick. However, in *The International Style*, the final Nick film, a coda reveals that Nick has retired from international spydom to a quiet domestic life in Greenland. He stands in the place of his father, by the backyard pool that was the site of his clash with Corny – now assimilated into the new world order. His new wife and baby sit nearby. Nick's face is expressive, for once, contorted in discomfort as he struggles to light the barbecue.

Oak, Ivy, and Other Dead Elms (1982)

Nick's second appearance, in *Oak, Ivy, and Other Dead Elms*, sees the character at college. He meets Brock (Peter Jordan, best known as host of the CBC series *It's a Living*), who embroils him in a preppie fraternity's neoconservative plans to transform campus into a fascistic throwback to the nostalgic past. Brock's dangerous nostalgia stems from childhood memories of the ravages of Dutch Elm disease, which plague his adulthood as nightmares. In an inversion of films like *Animal House* (1978), Nick pursues repression rather than release, and sides with Brock and his ilk: as Pevere notes, "in their stereotypical manner and matter, they are to Nick what Connie was to Billy: emblematic icons of a simpler time, when style, not substance, was all that mattered."[30]

Pevere's observation glosses over the fact that *style matters* to Paizs and to the film's aesthetic. Maddin appears as an extra in the film, and *Oak* bears the most similarities to Maddin's films: it is shot in black and white, features a feverish nightmare, and takes a complicated and self-reflexive stance on its own nostalgia (both formal/stylistic and on the level of content). Linda Hutcheon writes that "in the postmodern ... nostalgia itself gets both called up, exploited, *and* ironized."[31] *Oak* calls up, exploits, and ironizes nostalgia by presenting a plot in which Brock's nostalgia motivates him to run for student council. In the wake of his victory, this seemingly innocent longing for a nobler time in Balfour College history is transformed into a fascistic desire for control. Brock uses campus radio to rebroadcast old Glenn Miller programs, limits access to library books through censorious policies, and blocks attempts to set up a joint clinic and day care centre in favour of an old boys club. Brock's nostalgia does not just manifest itself in his preference for old media – Paizs presents this nostalgia through the film's production values. A further ironizing results, where the film seems to strike a critical pose in relation to Brock's nostalgia while indulging in its own. Shot in high-contrast black and white, with stylized acting, shadow scrims, and other elements of outdated film language, *Oak* reproduces antiquated cinema surfaces while Brock rebroadcasts Glenn Miller. The film invites us to view such nostalgic attempts to recapture the past as desperate and doomed. When Brock states, "Nothing is so far gone it cannot be lived – right here, right now!", the claim rings hollow, in ways that the disastrous development of the plot then echoes (Brock's attempt to return to the "innocent" past causes a handful of deaths, including his own).

Brock's enthusiasm for such things as the sugar cone ("There's never been a better idea!") also connects his nostalgia to the objects of consumer culture, and in fact it's possible to view nostalgia itself as a "product" meant to be consumed. As Steven Connor puts it, for a postmodern theorist like Fredric Jameson, "images, styles and representations are not the promotional accessories to economic products, they are the products themselves."[32] Much of the appeal of Paizs's films, and of Maddin's for that matter, lies in the recognition of anachronism and the pleasure it affords a viewer steeped in, and enamoured with, the forms and surfaces of cinema past. However, both filmmakers seem aware of and anxious about this nostalgic potential. Hutcheon writes that "our contemporary culture is indeed nostalgic; some parts of it – postmodern parts – are aware of the risks and lures of nostalgia, and seek to expose those through irony ... [but] from a postmodern point of view, the knowingness of this kind of irony may not be so much a defense against the power of nostalgia as the way in which nostalgia is made palatable today."[33] It is this ironic nostalgia, which operates on the level of the images and surfaces, that most connects the work of Paizs to the later work of Maddin. Both filmmakers routinely, albeit differently, employ anachronism in ways that acknowledge the toxic qualities of their appropriations.

Oak points forward to *Crime Wave* in Brock's transformation of the campus theatre, which begins to run pulp action fare like the (fictitious) throwback Second World War propaganda film *"A" Man Meets the Scourge.* In our sole glimpse of this supposed film, "A" Man bursts through a door, glances around, says, "Just as I thought – Japs!" and starts shooting. The similarity to Steven Penny's imagined Hollywood blockbuster, *The Last White Man in South Africa,* is hard to ignore (in our sole glimpse of that film, a soldier shouts "C'mon you bastards, I'm ready for ya!" and starts firing). In both instances a fictitious B-movie offering presents the dark underbelly of a character's desires, even as the character seems oblivious to the violent core of his own yearnings. The "A" Man movie clip nestles within the film's nostalgic style an anxious acknowledgment of the dangers of nostalgic appropriation, similar to the way that Maddin employs blackface in *Tales from the Gimli Hospital* (1988).

Nick's "quiet man" silence is maintained throughout *Oak*, despite being at odds with the film's genre and plot. While *Springtime* suggests motivations for Nick's silence – he appears alone in shots, apart from others, and the plot revolves around his inability to fulfil social expectations – Nick's silence in *Oak* seems more contrived and out-of-place, even though it appears unremarkable in the view of the other characters. As if aware of Nick's anachronistic status as a silent film star in the sound era, at one point Brock says of Nick, "Does he look like a squealer?" As well, in Brock's dying speech, he notices that Nick seems poised to say something but lets him off the hook: "Ssh, Nick – there's nothing left to say." This simple, sad nod to Nick's anachronistic silence exemplifies Paizs's ability to achieve immediate affect despite holding viewers at an ironic remove.

The International Style (1983)

Nick's final return (unless you count his reincarnation as Steven Penny) is in *The International Style*, which Cagle describes as a spy thriller "culled from the discarded excesses of 1950s drive-in and matinee fare."[34] Nick apparently majored in espionage at college. He breaks into "Starland," the mountain palace home of Quinton Frosst, who holds secret and powerful microtechnology that he plans to auction off to some government or supervillain once his sister Carmel is married off and out of his hair. (The connections with Maddin abound. John Harvie, who later starred as the son in Maddin's *The Dead Father*, plays Frosst. George Toles, screenwriter of Canada's first stop-motion animated feature, *Edison and Leo* [2008], and co-writer of numerous Maddin features, appears as a deranged count. Guy Maddin appears again, credited as "Gal Madden," in a small speaking role as a homicidal nurse.) Nick steals a rather large microchip (and thus, we presume, saves the world), and as an encore steals Carmel's heart. In its madcap tone, and its pastiche of styles and elements from various pulp genres, *International* most closely prefigures the aesthetic of *Crime Wave*.

International revels in its imitations and their unlikely combinations, offering a world that, as Cagle puts it, "is populated by wildly incongruous characters, including a dandy, his sister, an evil masseuse, assorted mafia types, crazed hillbillies, vaguely European villains, and their James-Bond-film-inspired henchmen."[35] The result, Pevere states, is a story set "in a universe totally governed by the dictates and skewed logic of pop convention."[36] Cagle captures the spirit of the film's overall tone, which "pulls together superficial elements from different genres and recombines them into a movie that, in its amazingly hybridized final form, is, as critic Umberto Eco has said of *Casablanca* [1942], not *a* movie, but 'the movies.'"[37] The film thus subordinates its interior concerns to this exterior theme: instead of *Obsession*'s (ahem) obsession with images and their potential to structure and cause desire, *International* offers its images in a gleeful rush.

Cagle reads this as an implicit critique of the Hollywood that Paizs imitates, noting that the film's title, "*The International Style*, suggests that the Hollywood styles appropriated by the film, together represent a collective 'international' style of film making designed, defined, and distributed by the American entertainment industry."[38] This argument better describes how Paizs's pastiche operates in *Crime Wave*, with its clear connection to the American entertainment industry (which Steven Penny dreams of dominating), than how pastiche operates in *International*, which seems to focus more on the representations *themselves* rather than on their global spread from, and continuing relation to, their source of issue. Cagle's reading also depends on viewing the events of *International*, and also of *Oak*, as part of "Nick's fantasy life."[39] Cagle justifies this reading by looking to the above-mentioned ending of *International*, in which Nick and his new wife return to the bucolic suburbia of *Springtime in Greenland*. For Cagle, "what this shot intimates, when taken in the context of the trilogy's overall structure, is that the plots of the second and third films are, in fact, part of a dream – the product of Nick's overactive and movie-addled imagination."[40]

This strange analytical move may be a reasonable interpretation, yet it seems unnecessary and has as its prime effect a deradicalizing of Paizs's postmodern approach. Viewing the events of *Oak* and *International* as the fantasy life of the character whose "real" life we then glimpse in *Springtime* smooths over the narrative disjuncture of the trilogy's story by subordinating sequences like "The House of Tomorrow" and almost the entirety of the other films to the world of Nick's Greenland "frame story." Being narratively subordinate, a segment like "The House of Tomorrow" also loses its ideological force. Cagle's interpretive move also ignores the fact that Nick's "conventional" and somewhat "realist" narrative (of poolside struggle, and stifled existence in

Greenland) is itself couched in the documentary-styled segments that open and close *Springtime*. Moreover, Cagle's analysis defuses the ontological uncertainty proper to *Crime Wave*, insofar as a similar uncertainty might appear in *The Three Worlds of Nick*, where the same unspeaking figure can transit through worlds both Technicolor and monochrome, populated by stereotypical males like Corny but also supervillains ripped from comic books. In effect, the postmodern emphasis on narrative worlds that have no fixed, stable ontological status, and their interpenetration by media surfaces, is abandoned for a modernist emphasis on epistemological uncertainty (these fantasy worlds revealing Nick's desires and point of view). Although both paths seem valid, and one suggests the other (as McHale notes, "push epistemological questions far enough and they 'tip over' into ontological questions,"[41] and vice versa), when the films themselves nod to their own artifice, they suggest their construction *as films*, not as Nick's fantasies. Thus, as McHale suggests of postmodernist narratives in general, "it is more *urgent* to interrogate [them] about [their] ontological implications."[42] In *Crime Wave*, a further collapse occurs, where film and fantasy appear coextensive.

Other aspects of *International* recall the earlier *Springtime* or prefigure *Crime Wave:* the framing narrator who poorly contextualizes the onscreen action, as if watching a different film ("the spirit of the evening will live on" he trumpets, as the wedding festivities descend into murder and rape); sudden eruptions of brutal violence (a cackling "Gal Madden" feeds an agent head-first into a furnace, then is later torn apart by dogs herself); and characters oblivious to their own strangeness, taking bizarre actions or spouting unnatural dialogue – here, as in the "House of Tomorrow" segment, we find blithe ideological statements that resemble commercial slogans ("We can take everything you need to make you happy and put it in a watch no bigger than this. Microtechnology: a big word making big changes small"). Even the narrator's insistence on the stunning varieties of cake available at the party hearkens back to Brock's praise of the sugar cone in *Oak* while also looking forward to the pyramid cake that symbolizes "The Top!" in Steven Penny's failed beginnings for "Crime Wave."

Crime Wave (1985)

On the strength of these short films, Paizs had become a major figure on Winnipeg's film scene and garnered national attention. In 1984, three of his shorts (*Obsession*, *Springtime*, and *International*) were screened at the Toronto Festival of Festivals as *John Paizs Trilogy*.[43] Now, the "John Paizs trilogy" is properly *The Three Worlds of Nick* and consists of the Nick films (*Springtime*, *Oak*, and *International*) that, in order, concern Nick's pre-college, college, and post-college days. Pevere writes of first viewing Paizs's films:

> You've got to understand what seeing John Paizs' short films was like back in '84. On the macro level, Canadian cinema was largely moribund. Although early stirrings of fresh life were evident in the first films of Egoyan, Bruce McDonald, Ron Mann and Peter Mettler, at that moment the concept of Canadian cinema was fraught with baggage. It remained beholden to the "documentary tradition," an inadvertently self-colonizing concept which yoked our filmmaking efforts to both an institutional history and stifling implications of standard practice and civic responsibility, and it had only begun to shrug off the dampening cloak of the tax-shelter binge, which saw dozens of faux-Hollywood features produced that featured past-prime American actors in movies that were barely, if ever, released ... Where the official versions of national cultural history tended to cling to documentary, scruffy realism, experimental cinema, high-minded McLarenesque animation and literary coming-of-age-tales set on oceanic prairies, Paizs' movies glommed onto far more fetchingly

> mundane influences: horror films and comics, hyper-square industrial films, '50s and '60s sitcom tropes, triple-bill spy movies and cleaning product commercials."[44]

Paizs also, to be clear, bears the influence of "documentary, scruffy realism, experimental cinema," and so forth, although his work subordinates the elements on Pevere's former list to the tropes of his latter list. In this way, Paizs continued to impress Pevere even though *Crime Wave*, in a way, *is* a "faux-Hollywood feature." Instead of copying Hollywood formulae (an effort doomed to failure in Canada, for the most part, due to relatively small budgets), Paizs copied the outdated surfaces of Hollywood in a manner that revealed their ideological underpinnings in a consumer culture – one in which these surfaces themselves had become available for consumption, copying, and (re)creation. *Crime Wave* is self-consciously faux-Hollywood, and its faux-Hollywood status becomes its subject.

By the time *John Paizs Trilogy* screened at the Toronto festival, Paizs had completed the script for *Crime Wave*. Earlier, like Steven Penny, Paizs had problems coming up with a workable concept. He wrote two failed feature scripts:

> I wrote an entirely different *Crime Wave*. It was a *Shoot the Piano Player* [1960] kind of thing, transplanted to Winnipeg. But I wasn't happy with it, so I wrote something else called *Crazy Casey*, about an 18-year-old girl who, based on a bad romantic experience, decides that being a young adult sucks, so she returns to childhood and starts to act like a 13-year-old. Living over her family's garage is this guy the same age as Casey, and he becomes romantically obsessed with her. The problem is she's like a child, and utterly in her own world ... I felt the pressure of ... having written two scripts that I wasn't happy with, and out of that came this idea about a guy who hasn't quite got it together as a screenwriter.[45]

Paizs then transformed his own general writing difficulties into Steven Penny's specific inability to write middles. Paizs also developed his "quiet man" character into a figure somewhere between Billy and Nick, in the sense that Paizs allows the viewer to glimpse some facets of Steven's inner life through the dramatization of his failed screenplay ideas.

Paizs's budget for *Crime Wave*, insofar as it can be reconstructed, consisted of two grants from the Canada Council for the Arts ($25,000 in 1983 and $17,000 in 1985), $15,000 from the Manitoba Arts Council, and $10,000 of Paizs's own money (including proceeds from the sale of his car).[46] This puts the initial budget at $67,000 – Paizs received a further $10,000 to $15,000 from Manitoba Film and Sound to reshoot the film's ending, putting the total budget between $77,000 and $82,000. However, he neglected to keep precise records, and various total budgets between $70,000 and $100,000 have been reported in the press. Whatever the precise budget, it was minuscule compared to most feature film budgets, and a testament to Paizs's ingenuity and resourcefulness given the ambition of *Crime Wave*, which involves numerous car chases, many locations and actors, multiple constructed sets, overturned vehicles, and detailed *mise en scène*. "Shot on location in Winnipeg, Southern Manitoba and the Favorite Pictures Studios, 1984–86," as the credits announce, the film is a decidedly home-made affair (Paizs is a self-taught filmmaker). However, in contrast to the intentional primitivism of Maddin, the aesthetic of *Crime Wave* is Technicolor Hollywood, albeit its unfashionable, low-budget pulp offerings.

Much anticipated by the time of its completion, *Crime Wave* premiered at the Toronto Festival in September 1985 – on Friday the 13th, doomed from the beginning, it seems. Pevere remembers that "for the first two-thirds of its running time, *Crime Wave* played like a dream. The audience roared with laughter ... and you could hear gasps of approving amazement over certain scenes ... What happened next also felt like a dream, although of a decidedly different kind. The projection

Tom Fijal on home-made rigging – a good example of Paizs's independent, low-budget, "low-tech" approach to filmmaking. Courtesy of John Paizs, from the director's personal collection.

suddenly stopped, the audio groaned to silence, and the lights went up."[47] Perhaps foreboding *Crime Wave*'s eventual fate, a malfunction had caused the screening to stop for ten to twenty minutes. This interruption occurred near the film's end, just as its tone was shifting towards a darker, less comedic register. This tonal shift, coupled with the delay, caused the film to lose the audience: Pevere recalls that "it was like a different *Crime Wave* entirely had snuck in and taken the original's place."[48] Paizs reacted with disappointment and dejection:

> I remember going back to my hotel room afterwards feeling like the film had screened poorly, even though it had gone over great up until the malfunction. But I was in a very kind of susceptible state of mind. I had literally worked day and night to get the film ready in time for the festival and had actually picked up the print fresh off the printer from the lab on my way to the airport, no time to check it. And I was exhausted. And after the malfunction and the tonally very different old ending and far fewer laughs, I just sort of crashed.[49]

Despite the poor screening, the next day film critic John Harkness called Paizs at his hotel and asked him to breakfast. Harkness praised *Crime Wave* but told Paizs he would not be writing about the film because Paizs had not yet secured distribution.[50] Jay Scott's review in the *Globe and Mail* also praised the film. "If the great Canadian comedy ever gets made," Scott began, "[then] John Paizs ... may be the filmmaker to do it."[51] On the whole, Scott's review of *Crime Wave* was positive, although he criticized its ending: "unlike his alter ego Steven, [Paizs has] got beginnings and middles: all he needs to learn is how to end it all."[52]

Paizs "was soon thinking it would be worth it to redo the last 20 minutes of the film, to make it more like the rest of the film, faster and funnier basically."[53] One imagines a young Paizs fixating on Scott's "if" – on the fact that Scott had located the "great Canadian comedy" in the speculative future, rather than recognizing its appearance as *Crime Wave*. Spurred by this review and by his own growing dissatisfaction with the film's ending, Paizs withdrew the film from circulation. He wrote and shot a new ending over the following months: "as it turned out, that premiere was like a premiere and a test screening rolled into one."[54] Although reworking large segments of a film is common in Hollywood, the practice is much less common for cash-strapped independent productions. Greg Klymkiw, former Director of Marketing for the Winnipeg Film Group (where he worked with many filmmakers, including Paizs, and shepherded Maddin's early career) and now the Producer-in-Residence at the Canadian Film Centre, describes Paizs's decision as "a very brave move for someone who had no money."[55]

An unfortunate effect of Paizs's decision to reshoot the film's ending was the loss of any momentum the film might have had in the wake of its initial, positive reviews. Paizs recalls thinking "that a sale of the film might depend on [reshooting the ending], or that I could make an even better sale if I did."[56] Perhaps he was correct: not just Scott, but *Variety* "noted the film's weak conclusion" (reported the *Winnipeg Sun*), although *Variety* also "said the movie was [otherwise] a triumph."[57] The *Variety* review praised "Paizs' wizardry [as] the achievement of a hyperkinetic humour and pungent vignettes" and claimed that *Crime Wave* was "guaranteed to regale festival crowds and has a quirky potential if developed as a cult or midnight movie."[58]

Crime Wave's contemporaneous commercial potential will remain a mystery, because the film was not thus cultivated. Yet it did develop its own cult following in the ensuing decades, even spawning the song "Crimewave" by Who Shot Hollywood (its lyrics are all quotes from Paizs's film) on a 2008 EP titled *Springtime in Greenland*. A 2004 article in *Take One* declared *Crime Wave* one of the Top 10 debut features in Canadian cinema history,[59] although the film remains unavailable through traditional channels and Paizs is not well known. By the time its new ending was affixed, interest in the film had waned, although *Variety* reports that *Crime Wave* premiered in its new form in Vancouver on 21 March 1986, during a National Film Week screening, and later played at the Vancouver International Film Festival.[60] In another spell of bad luck, the new Pacific Cine Centre was broken into that night. Theatre staff made sure to clarify that Paizs had not incited the crime: "the movie *Crime Wave* was an [80]-minute comedy ... the break-in was an unfortunate coincidence."[61]

Next, Paizs secured a distribution deal with Norstar Releasing. At the time, this deal was seen as positive not only for Paizs but also for the entire Winnipeg film community. In December 1986 the *Winnipeg Free Press* reported on the then-pending deal: "[Carmen] Katz [then the executive director of the Winnipeg Film Group] says the big-chain coup bodes well for other independently made local films. 'It will give credibility to those wanting to make feature-length, cultural films for widespread distribution.' ... 'John will be laughing for his next film,' [Grant] Guy [a spokesman for the Winnipeg Film Group] said. 'Already we've had feelers from the U.S. and Canada from people wanting to commit money now hoping for part of the return.'"[62] Such professions of faith are heartbreaking in retrospect, now that we know Paizs did not produce a follow-up film. The same *Winnipeg Free Press* article ends on a sober note more in keeping with *Crime Wave*'s eventual fate: "How is Paizs reacting to all the fuss? Just the way you might expect an artist to: he literally can't afford to be affected by it. 'John is working for the city traffic department for 10 weeks,' Katz said. 'He has to pay the rent.'"[63] A month later, while *Crime Wave* was screening at film festivals in the United States, the *Globe and Mail* reported that "Less than a week after the U.S. premiere of his first feature film, Winnipeg director John Paizs is waiting anxiously for a cheque from the Unemployment Insurance Commission."[64]

Norstar did not capitalize on the independent cinema market, instead brokering a home video release. In the United States the film was retitled *The Big Crime Wave* to avoid confusion with Sam Raimi's *Crimewave* (1985). A loophole in Paizs's contract stipulated that he would not be paid by the company until after the film's theatrical release, and without a theatrical release Paizs found himself without money. Eventually, *Crime Wave* played on screens in Winnipeg, and it has since been screened occasionally at festivals and in retrospectives. In the original agreement with Norstar, Paizs retained the rights to distribute the 16mm print of the film, which is still handled by the Winnipeg Film Group. Paizs's strained relationship with Norstar Releasing ended in the worst possible manner: Norstar collapsed, bankrupt, and was purchased by Alliance Atlantis (later Alliance Films, and now folded into the Entertainment One or eOne group). In the process, as is common in cases of bankruptcy, all of Norstar's assets were acquired by Alliance, including *Crime Wave*. Unfortunately, perhaps because it had acquired the film by accident, Alliance showed no interest in marketing or distributing it. (eOne completed its purchase of Alliance in January 2013,[65] and at the time of writing it is too early to say what, if anything, this might mean for *Crime Wave*.) According to Paizs, two companies had made unsuccessful attempts to wrest the film from Alliance for a DVD release:

> The first was in about 2005, and Alliance would only go along if the company (based in California) agreed to licence a number of Alliance titles, including *Crime Wave*, in a package deal. The company declined. The second attempt was [in 2011] ... Alliance reacted with surprise that they even owned this film they never heard of ... their answer this second time was that they had just sold the U.S. rights to *Crime Wave* (as part of a package deal) to a U.S. company and that any deal would have to be made with them. That was attempted but never reached fruition (not quite sure why ...).[66]

The rights to *Crime Wave* continue to be randomly or accidentally exploited, while illegal Internet file sharing of degraded copies stands as the film's main distribution channel. The Hollywood cliché of "development Hell" might be apt if rephrased here: *Crime Wave* languishes in "distribution Hell" even today.

After *Crime Wave*

Although demoralized, Paizs wrote a number of follow-up features after *Crime Wave*, but "a couple of them proved too big to get off the ground and one of them I lost faith in the subject matter."[67] Paizs had also decided to retire his "quiet man" character and change his artistic direction, but he had not yet found this new direction. He was offered a job directing *Palais Royale* (1988) but turned it down, and he almost directed *Perfectly Normal* (1991).[68] Meanwhile *Crime Wave* began to develop a cult following through its VHS release and occasional appearances on late night television. As *Crime Wave*'s reputation grew, Bruce McCulloch saw the film and hired Paizs to direct for *The Kids in the Hall*'s second season. Paizs directed about a quarter of that season's filmed segments, including those featuring Dave Foley's "M Piedlourde" (Mr Heavyfoot) character: Piedlourde is another "quiet man," a silent-film character seemingly inspired by Jacques Tati.

Paizs moved from Winnipeg to Toronto while pursuing this new television career, and directed for other shows, including *Maniac Mansion*. In 1995 he moved back to Winnipeg "after the comedy directing scene pretty much dried up"; by then he had been selling "window cleaning door to door in Toronto for a few months."[69] He "considered giving up on film, or at least diversifying, and enrolled at the Applied Multimedia Training Centre to learn computer graphics."[70] Instead of diversifying, after Paizs graduated he was able to resume his television career, directing commercials as well as episodes for shows such as *The*

Adventures of Shirley Holmes and *John Woo's Once a Thief*. Paizs became the Director-in-Residence at the Canadian Film Centre in 2000, and moved back to Toronto in 2002.[71]

Paizs had taken a long, circuitous route to directing his sophomore feature, fourteen years after his first. Writers Phil Bedard and Larry Lalonde, like Bruce McCulloch, had seen *Crime Wave* on late night television, and hired Paizs to direct *Top of the Food Chain* (1999), a parody of science fiction B-movies with distinctly Paizs-like themes. The film takes place in the small town of Exceptional Vista, in the "western central northeast" (of, we assume, Ontario). The economy of Exceptional Vista has been devastated by the explosion of the local nut factory, which has caused most citizens to flee. Those who remain fill their days with fishing, perverse sex, alchemy, and American television. On the upside, the local women's club has discovered how to turn rocks to gold and resurrect the dead. On the downside, the town's most eligible bachelorette, Sandy Fawkes, is in an incestuous relationship with her brother Guy Fawkes, and strange creatures have begun eating people in the "lumpy, bumpy part of town outside of town." Worse still, the town has lost its television reception. The world-famous atomic scientist Carol Lamonte, who has come to vacation in town, sets out to uncover the interconnected mysteries of precisely what is eating the townspeople and why they can't get any good channels. Although conventional in form (Paizs abandoned the mannered pastiche of his 1980s films for a generic style), in its content *Top of the Food Chain* shares some elements with *Crime Wave*, in that it brims with B-movie science fiction and horror tropes. Paizs's initial reaction on reading the script nicely conveys the film's bizarre tone: "it was like a cross between *Alien* [1979], *Petticoat Junction* and *The Naked Gun* [1988]."[72] Like *Crime Wave*, the film was retitled for its U.S. home video release, as *Invasion!*

Paizs's next feature film, *Marker* (2005), is a less successful blending of genres. Although also lacking a pastiche aesthetic, it attempts to graft a horror film plot onto a small-town coming-of-age story. As Sylvia matures, she begins to undergo bodily transformations; soon after, she discovers that some of the women in her town have likewise grown horns and become goat-like. Apparently a female satyr, Sylvia struggles with her growing sexual urges and the prejudices of the townspeople, in particular the men. Paizs has noted his failure to achieve "any atmosphere" of horror in the film: "all I really could do was to get the bare bones, and not even all of them."[73] The protagonist responds to developments with disgust and fright – which seemingly aligns *Marker* with the genre of body horror – but quickly accepts her lot and even develops pride in her new horns. Thus *Marker* becomes a feminist tale of defiance, with the protagonist's increasing self-possession defusing any horror. Unlike Paizs's other films, which ground themselves in ironic comedy, *Marker* displays no irony in its reproduction of horror film clichés, and contains few jokes (despite a hilarious moment when one character turns to stare down a taxidermied duck).

Crime Wave marks the apex of Paizs's artistic development. It was also his last foray as a writer-director. Notwithstanding the strengths found in his later work as a director – for example, in *Top of the Food Chain* – his career as a filmmaker seems to have ended with *Crime Wave*. Paizs himself has advanced this view: "I actually made my last film before [Maddin] made his first. When I say my last film I mean the last that I both wrote and directed, that can rightly be called mine."[74] Although still a working director, Paizs does not seem to be poised for a return to personal filmmaking. In a 2007 interview, he defended this decision:

> Most filmmakers who are able to keep their own particular thing going are by and large remaking the same film over and over. But I decided I wanted to pull the plug on what I was doing. I could have kept going – I had more ideas for silent man films, I even had a kind of sequel to *Crime Wave*, but I stopped myself. It wasn't that I was creatively dried

> up or couldn't get money, it was because after nobody would play *Crime Wave*, even as a midnight movie, I figured I wasn't going to get where I wanted to go by doing the silent man thing. Festivals may like it, but that's where it was going to end. I was very ambitious at the time, and I wanted my films to play at the local theatre. I made some choices that probably set the occasionally bumpy road of my career, post-*Crime Wave* ... but I didn't see that I had a choice. And I still don't think I had one.[75]

We might view this "early retirement" from personal filmmaking as not just a commercial but an artistic choice. Certainly, it seems in keeping with Paizs's decision to reshoot the ending of *Crime Wave* rather than let it proceed on the festival circuit with a flawed ending despite positive reviews and reactions. This line of thinking refuses to cast Paizs in the victim's role – as sufferer of bad luck and bad business deals – and allows us to view his 1980s work as the culmination of a significant oeuvre rather than the arbitrary terminus of a career cut short. The films of John Paizs – especially *Crime Wave*, the logical end of his artistic project – deserve consideration apart from the circumstances of their production, even though they exemplify the historical trend of 1980s Canadian postmodernism.

3

The Greatest Color Crime Movie Never Made

As *Crime Wave* begins, the opening credits introduce a number of its overarching themes. The Americanized spelling of the production company, "Favorite Pictures," may speak to Paizs's own ambitions for a U.S. release, but it also seems appropriate for a film that wants, at its core, to be a Hollywood film. *Crime Wave* both loves and loathes Hollywood convention, and these conflicting impulses inform its pastiche aesthetic. While reaching for the lost glory of Hollywood's bygone era – albeit that of B-movies and other commercial fare rather than the "classics" – Paizs recovers but also ridicules the cast-offs of American cinema by reproducing stylistic aspects and story elements from various "paracinemas." That term, coined by Jeffrey Sconce, refers to film genres and traditions that exist outside the Hollywood mainstream and that lack a certain cultural legitimacy, and also to a critical strategy for approaching those films.[1]

Much criticism has devoted itself to legitimating paracinematic fare, but the term itself contains the suggestion that these cinema traditions stand in parasitic relation to film's cultural mainstream. *Crime Wave* thematizes this parasitic relation by resorting to a pastiche of paracinematic forms to tell the story of a filmmaker who desires to craft a Hollywood film that will out-Hollywood Hollywood film. This effort is doomed, like a parasite without a host, since it demands either a film made within the Hollywood system (which Steven cannot access, as a down-and-out Canadian) or one made in direct opposition to Hollywood cinema. Any such film would unintentionally affirm and reinscribe the dominance of Hollywood, since its revolution would have no meaning otherwise – as a thing resisted, Hollywood remains a thing of power. The paracinematic surfaces and metafictional structure of *Crime Wave* together suggest that Steven's project must fail, thus undercutting his fantasy of success.

Wherefore Art Thou *Crime Wave*?

The unsubtle title *Crime Wave*, and the dramatic music that underscores its title card (which Paizs "hand-painted onto animation cels"),[2] grounds the film's genre: *Crime Wave* is one of the "color crime pictures" that Steven Penny loves. "Color crime" is a fictional genre invented by Paizs, a coined term that seems appropriate to 1950s pulp thrillers and that suggests the reverse of the term "film noir." Paizs also apes the opening credits and title cards of these 1950s thrillers, while parodying Hollywood's frenetic marketing terms. The title cards declare that *Crime Wave* has been "produced in Totalcolor/Selectosound and Ultra-Focus." "Totalcolor" spoofs "Technicolor": for Paizs, "shooting Technicolor wasn't an option [so] I mimicked the look by lighting with hard light, which is what they mainly used when they shot Technicolor. Hard light creates high contrast and saturates colours to make them pop. For exteriors I lit with direct, unfiltered sunlight, which of course is also hard light."[3] "Selectosound" suits the film's soundscape. Paizs replaced or added sound in post-production, taking the selective use of sound in radio dramas as his aural inspiration.[4] Even though these created terms describe the film's aesthetic approach to sound and colour, on another level "Totalcolor" is a parodic joke, like "Ultra-Focus." The latter term, although absurd, seems appropriate: whatever depth appears in *Crime*

Wave, Paizs focuses attention on the surface, to highlight forms with ironic playfulness.

Paizs's title also misdirects: just as Steven Penny's film "Crime Wave" promises a lurid wave of sensational crimes but doesn't deliver (due to his failure to complete its script), *Crime Wave*'s plot does not concern crime (unless we count Dr Jolly's spree of sex murder, which is suggested but not seen). Instead, *Crime Wave* focuses on Steven's struggle to write a script for "Crime Wave" and his frustrations during this artistic process. This auteurist focus might suggest that we read the title *Crime Wave* as some transformation of the term "New Wave," despite the film's lack of otherwise overt connections to either the musical genre or the varied films of *La Nouvelle Vague*.

Paizs doesn't recall intending the title in this way, but imagines that he might have been influenced by the French New Wave as far as the title is concerned, since "*Breathless* [1960] and *Shoot the Piano Player* [1960] were huge touchstones for me. They were auteurist pictures that set the standard for cool, [and] sourced so much of what I was sourcing from Hollywood, especially Poverty Row productions, and all with a DIY aesthetic that put picture-making within reach of practically anyone with a Bolex (especially *Breathless*). In fact, it might not be too farfetched to say that, along with *Pink Flamingos* [1972], they may very well have, in a larger sense, pointed the way."[5] Paizs remembers "a weekly cinema night that the [University of Manitoba's] Med students union used to put on back in the late '70s at a theatre at the hospital on William [Avenue]"[6] (Winnipeg's Health Sciences Centre). That is where Paizs first saw films like *Pink Flamingos* and *Reefer Madness* (1936). He remembers being struck, in particular, by the "tabloid style"[7] of the narration in *Pink Flamingos* (which may have influenced the mannered narration of Paizs's own films). Paizs connects Waters's tabloid style and "revelling in bad taste" with the style of "Steven's initial beginnings and endings."[8] Also, the enjoyment of cult films like *Reefer Madness* depends on ironic detachment, one of the fundamental techniques in Paizs's toolbox. In any case, reading *Crime Wave* as a declaration of intent, as a manifesto for a movement that never materialized, seems productive and appropriate, given the lofty ambitions of both Penny and Paizs. Nevertheless, the dramatic music of the opening credits seems odd and inappropriate – a false promise, like Steven's own self-promise to craft the greatest color crime movie of all time.

Likewise, crass promises of "Totalcolor," "Selectosound," and "Ultra-Focus" do not seem relevant to a metafiction about the artistic process; they are more fitting as preface to a crime drama. In fact, *Crime Wave*'s plot does feature a number of violent crimes, although most of them occur in the imagined beginnings and endings of Steven's "Crime Wave" script. These eruptions of violence get played for laughs, yet a darker and more serious core of violence lurks beneath them and throughout *Crime Wave*, so that the title might be read ironically (the film promising but not delivering a crime wave), descriptively (it's a film about a film called "Crime Wave," after all), or self-reflexively (the film itself constitutes a series of crimes, through its conceptual violence) – among other possibilities.

We might wonder: To what film do these opening credits belong? To John Paizs's *Crime Wave* or to Steven Penny's "Crime Wave"? To both at the same time? Since Paizs and Penny are conflated to some degree, and since we'll be encouraged later in the film to consider Paizs's *Crime Wave* as a co-production by Steven and his young friend Kim, these are fair questions. Paizs sets up and plays with audience expectations through this initial credit sequence, and these set-ups pay off, covertly, in metafictional gags and flourishes as the film progresses. In contrast to the later *Adaptation*, which stresses its own development through organic, self-directed processes (its metafiction is a metaphor for the process of adaptive evolution), *Crime Wave* emphasizes its status as a created thing (through aggressive insistence on its own artifice).

This credit sequence is followed by the first beginning of "Crime Wave," the film-within-a-film that Steven Penny attempts to write. All at once, we're thrown into a world of excess, a dreamworld where fantasies play out in conventional Hollywood fashion. "The Top! Few guys made it!", shrieks the narrator, as a cake in the shape of a pyramid, but bearing a map of the world on its icing, spins. This cake seems a seductive if silly symbol of world domination, complete with a cherry on top. Although we cannot know to look at it, the cake is also hollow: "cake icing over a cardboard pyramid shell" that Paizs's mother helped him make (a different cake from the one shared by Steven and Kim at the film's end, which we can see is "cake all the way through").[9] The narrator's enthusiasm heightens the absurdity of this cake-globe. He clearly believes that this cake sums it all up, so from the first moments of the film we're struck by twinned disconnections: between what we see and what the narrator seems to see, and between what Steven considers to be a normal, reasonable desire and what we might view as frantic, panicked insanity. (Unknown to the audience, these disconnections resonate even in the production process itself: the real cake and the dreamed cake aren't the same, although in this example Steven gets to have his hollow, fantasy cake and eat his real cake too.) A darkness shimmers beneath *Crime Wave*'s colourful surface, and although not yet apparent, this cake crests the tip of that iceberg. In its pyramid shape, death-like, it presents Steven's dream as a tomb.

Although Christopher Harris has praised Steven Penny for having "a beautifully sick mind," noting that "his rejected scripts ferociously satirize"[10] various aspects of American culture, we should be clear on the division of labour here. Paizs may mock and satirize, but Steven writes with earnestness. He realizes the weakness of what he writes, discarding his scripts, but he then writes the same thing again – three times in the film's beginning. Not until the final beginning and ending does Steven seem to recognize the scope of his failure and hold himself at a distance, for scrutiny. We might also ask what is being satirized. The obvious answer – popular culture in general and Hollywood movies in particular – is arguably the target of Paizs's own satire (although, in mimicry, Paizs also flatters), but it is not Steven Penny's target. Rather, Steven's initial torments result from his inability to follow in Hollywood's footsteps. Only later, in his final beginning and ending, does he view with horror the possibility that he might realize this dream.

Steven's initial ignorance of the badness of his early scripts (he considers them failures, but by the second beginning and ending we know he doesn't understand *how* they are failures) is consistent with a basic tactic in comedy. The comic figure takes his own plight seriously, even though we consider his plight absurd: once the comic figure laughs at himself, the joke isn't funny any more (for us). In *Crime Wave* this comic disparity grows (best exemplified by the seeming cluelessness of the "Crime Wave" narrator), the gap widening until it begins to bend back on itself. As the film's situations become more comic, they develop dark, painful shadows that deepen into pathos and melancholy. Yet even in these darker moments, *Crime Wave* maintains its obsession with pop-culture surfaces. The most succinct illustration of Paizs's sensibilities is found *outside* the film, on the title page of the original typed screenplay for *Crime Wave*, dated March 1984. Paizs has photocopied a picture of a small dog below the film's title. The photo caption reads: "Marilyn Monroe's little dog, Moff, being led out of her house after she was found dead in her bedroom."[11]

Beginning the Fantasy

"The Top" that few guys make it to, in the context of this first film-within-a-film beginning's diegesis, is the "big time tribute racket" that has been "pretty well sewed up" by three big "operators." Another comic disparity is established here: the distance between the megalomaniacal rhetoric of world domination embedded in the cake-globe-pyramid image and the narrator's rabid foaming, and the parochial nature of these "big time rackets." In introducing the first "operator," Eddie Carlton and his "Tribute to Buddy," Paizs also establishes one of the film's basic postmodern concerns: a lack of difference or meaningful distinction between the real and the unreal.

Even though Eddie begins each performance with a nod to "the real Buddy in Heaven" and his gig poster declares (with an arrow pointing to Carlton's picture) that "this is *not* the real Buddy!" the narrator states that "scores of female fans too young to remember declared that Eddie was the one and only." Paizs neither supports the maintenance of such distinctions by focusing on the audience's error in a cultural critique nor celebrates this collapse of the authentic and fake into a single amorphous mass. Instead, Paizs focuses on the anxiety that this collapse produces for his protagonist, Steven Penny, who is tortured by the clear and insurmountable difference between reality and fantasy.

Steven's anxious relation to his own fantasy of completing "Crime Wave" and achieving world-wide color crime movie domination finds its ultimate expression in his final beginning and ending to "Crime Wave," but at this juncture it's important to note the salience of Steven's status as the screenwriter of the fantasized "Crime Wave," and thus as an active if not always aware author of his own fantasy. Throughout *Crime Wave*, Steven's attempts to write "Crime Wave" find him failing and then repeating the gesture. Žižek notes that "When ... the subject actually experiences a series of phantasmatic formations which interrelate as so many permutations of each other, this series is never complete: it is always as if the actually experienced series presents so many variations on some underlying 'fundamental' fantasy which is *never* actually experienced by the subject."[12] Steven's permutations of "Crime Wave" seem to draw him closer and closer to the point of grasping the fantasy, but what he finally seems to grasp instead is the neces-

"Tribute Artists" from Steven Penny's first beginning to "Crime Wave." Zal Saper as Buddy Holly (top left), Neil Lawrie as Leonard "Hank" Taylor (top right), Mark Yuill as Sid Vicious (bottom left), and Darrell Baran as Ronnie Boyles (bottom right). Courtesy of John Paizs, from the director's personal collection.

sary incompleteness of this series (the impossibility of "Crime Wave," the reality of its lack).

Paizs makes an unusual, postmodern move in the next sequence, as the narrator introduces the second tribute legend, Leonard "Hank" Taylor. The actor playing Hank, Neil Lawrie, like other actors in the film (and in many independent films), recurs again in a later role (as Dr Jolly). What's unusual or disconcerting about his reappearance is that no attempt whatsoever will be made to differentiate the two characters visually: Lawrie even wears the same distinctive cowboy hat in both roles. Hank's recurrence as Jolly thus produces a recursion. As Hank, Lawrie appears in Steven's "Crime Wave," the fictional film-within-a-film, but in the later appearance as Dr Jolly, Lawrie appears in Steven's "reality" (in the diegesis of Paizs's own *Crime Wave*). Thus, as Lawrie moves from one character to another, he also moves from one diegetic reality to another, undermining their possible separation. The status of reality within the film is quite complicated even without this move; whether this easy re-recognition of Lawrie by the audience occurs or does not, the prefiguring of Dr Jolly in Leonard "Hank" Taylor suggests that Steven later summons Jolly from his imaginings, just as he now summons Hank. The further suggestion is that Steven's later encounter with Jolly does not play out in "reality" but within another fantasy realm. Since the "Kansas" of the film is a bizarre environment shot through with science fiction tropes, this interpretation seems to gain support from within the film. However, we should avoid the temptation to consider the absurd twists that occur later in the film to be "mere" fantasy (just as we turned from this particular aspect of Cagle's similar interpretation of *The Three Worlds of Nick*). Andrew Gibson suggests that, in general but especially in postmodern texts, the "geometric" separation of narrative levels is a function of a flawed narratology rather than a quality of literature and film: "narrative levels ... are always in hybridised or composite relations with each other ... [that] subject the levels themselves to constant modification."[13] The narrative worlds within *Crime Wave* seem at first separate, but they develop absurd interrelations, undercutting the critical tendency to view one part of the film's reality as more or less "real" than the others.

Crime Wave operates not just to present itself as "Crime Wave" but to insist on this presentation as a lie. Penny's dreamed film, "Crime Wave," is produced within *Crime Wave* (in its filmed beginnings and endings) but at the same time is located elsewhere, in some impossible, fantasized space that eludes all of its intermixed narrative levels. *Crime Wave,* then, points to the absolute impossibility and non-existence of this fantasy "Crime Wave," focusing not on "the dream" that deludes its heroes from the North but rather on the gap it cannot fill. The situation here recalls another "blocked writer" film, *Barton Fink* (1991). A postcard featuring a woman at the beach is pinned to the wall of Barton Fink's hotel/office throughout the film. At its end, as Barton sits on the beach, he sees this precise image replicated in reality. Either Barton has lost the ability to distinguish reality from fiction, and is fantasizing her appearance, or the film *Barton Fink* has refused to sustain such internal distinctions. Since *Barton Fink* also features a screenwriter trying to craft the best script ever in a fictional, paracinematic genre (the wrestling picture), and culminates in a showdown with a serial killer, we might suspect the Coen Brothers of having seen *Crime Wave*. In fact, years prior to the appearance of *Barton Fink*, the Coens were sent a copy of *Crime Wave* by Norstar "to see whether they would have any advice as to cutting the third reel,"[14] although it is not known whether they viewed or were influenced by Paizs's film. In any case, throughout *Crime Wave,* it is implied that no "reality" exists anywhere, in any meaningful sense, and that Steven Penny lives entirely within a self-generated fantasy space. We might take this on the literal, metafictional level, since Steven is a character in Paizs's film, but it also works on a figural, thematic level, since Steven's desire outstrips his imagination, so that his fantasy eventually becomes unsatisfactory on all levels.

A New Narrator, in a … Documentary?

With the appearance of the final tribute artist, Patrick Nelson and his tribute to "Sid," the narrator confirms the stranglehold these three have on the tribute "racket" while inscribing the importance of fantasy in these filmic, well, fantasies. This first beginning and ending also sets the formula for Steven's subsequent beginnings and endings. First, a "racket" controlled in the East, South, and West by three big-time "operators" creates a situation where "new talent had it tough breaking in." Then, "from the North," a new talent proceeds to "smash the order" and dominate the industry anyway. "His name," in this first instance, is Ronnie Boyles. He stands proud while a "sunburst effect" flickers in the background – this effect has been "airbrushed by [Paizs] onto animation paper, then photographed on an animation stand onto film which had already been exposed with the actors, creating double exposures."[15] Like Steven himself, and his later imagined heroes from the North (all with sunbursts signalling their glory, and all of whom seem like stand-ins for Penny just as Penny seems like a stand-in for Paizs), "he had a dream."

All begins with a dream, and the dream makes all possible. But in each instance, it is really acts of murderous violence that make the ascension of these would-be stars possible. Ronnie pursues his dream, but fails – the dream doesn't materialize as planned, and he's unable to cope with any setbacks. That's "an actual salami"[16] in his pants – he's not really happy to see you – he's a fake, through and through, a mere copier rather than an esteemed "tribute artist," and he cannot even come up with five dollars for the PA rental. Ronnie soon sees violence as a remedy for his desperate situation, murdering the club owner who gave him his first break. Here Steven begins to deliver on the promise of the title "Crime Wave": Ronnie Boyles's rise to prominence within the tribute racket comes not through service and sacrifice to his dream but as the result of an implied series of violent crimes that he commits.

This dark undercurrent of violence is undermined as soon as it is established, by the appearance of a new narrator, Kim. In contrast to the slick, bombastic narrator of Steven Penny's "Crime Wave," the preteen Kim brims with awkward innocence. Played by Eva Kovacs, Kim possesses a charming naivety that goes a long way towards making *Crime Wave* work. Just as Paizs manages to meld the disparate aesthetics of exploitative B-movies and guileless educational films by processing them all through a singular vision, so Kim-as-narrator serves to render *Crime Wave*'s violence and sexuality comic through her Disney-movie purity (a purity echoed, perhaps, in the snow falling outside her window). A subversive rather than a safe procedure: if *Crime Wave* "manages to be both the blackest of black comedies and the most light-hearted of spoofs,"[17] then Kim's character sutures these structures (to return to the snow: we should remember that, like most of the world that we see on the cinema's screen, it's not real – in this case, "plastic snow purchased at Malabar's [a Winnipeg costume house]" – its purity a lie).[18] Paizs cast Kovacs as Kim after meeting her at a Hungarian function, where she dressed as a bug and read a poem about having six legs.[19] Kovacs remembers having an honest lack of awareness about *Crime Wave*'s unsavoury elements: the script "always arrived in handwritten form in pieces. Just the stuff that pertained to me and the lines I had to memorize ... I had no idea what all the other actors' scenes were all about.'[20]

In the context of a first viewing, the audience doesn't yet know who Kim is or why she's suddenly replaced our overblown narrator, literally finishing his sentence. Only when Kim explains herself does the viewer realize that what has appeared so far is the first beginning to Steven

Penny's "Crime Wave." Steven is thus introduced by Kim prior to his appearance on-screen, which places further distance between the writer-director-protagonist and his ostensible audience. Kim establishes her own relationship to Steven by noting that this beginning was written on the back of the rent papers supplied by her father. She explains that the room in which she stands (with its color crime movie poster wallpapering, reminiscent of the "images and surfaces" that litter Billy Botski's domicile) was where Steven wrote the just-seen beginning. Its ending, Kim notes without sarcasm, was written on the next page.

Although the film dives right into this ending, we should note that within four minutes Paizs has both established the metafictional structure of his film-within-a-film and complicated that structure by introducing Kim. Ostensibly, the film has claimed at least two genres by this point: the "color crime movie" – pure Hollywood – and the documentary – pure National Film Board. Both claims seem illusory, impure at best. It has become common to speak, as Zoë Druick puts it, of a "binary ... between documentary and fiction – reality and invention," whose admixture creates "two distinct hybrid forms ... mockumentary, a combination of documentary form and fictional content, and docudrama, a mix of fictional form with documentary content."[21] Postmodern thought troubles even this basic, commonsensical distinction, by positing reality as an invention, while psychoanalysis similarly considers reality subjective, dependent on disavowed fantasy structures.

The collapse of such distinctions is suggested by *Crime Wave*'s complex metafictional structure. By presenting Kim in a "real world" location significant to Penny's story, providing "the facts" of his biography like a news personality (as it happens, later in life, Eva Kovacs became a well-known broadcaster on Winnipeg's Global TV), Paizs also drops a thread he will pick up at the film's conclusion: the suggestion that John Paizs's *Crime Wave*, within which Steven Penny's "Crime Wave" is framed, is in fact a film co-produced by Kim and Steven (adding another fold to Paizs's metafiction). Stylistically, then, it seems both natural and appropriate that *Crime Wave* at once resembles both a 1950s pulp thriller and a school safety film. What we seem to have in *Crime Wave* is a mockumentary, but if Kim and Steven have produced a documentary about Steven's struggle, in lieu of or even *as* "Crime Wave," then perhaps we have a docudrama as well. What do we view in the scenes that constitute the "primary" diegesis (the parts that seem most like a "movie")? Do we have direct access to events as they occur, or do we watch Kim and Steven re-enacting earlier scenes, as her voice-over narration suggests? A film reveals itself to be a film-within-a-film that itself is a docudrama inside of a mockumentary that is supposed to be a "color crime movie" that is about its own production although it has not been produced, unless of course it was and this is it, but in any case it's also a fictional art film comedy ... *Crime Wave* (which has barely begun!) has already thrown itself into chaos, and any possible, meaningful distinction between reality and invention has collapsed.

Mary Ann Doane has noted how "in the documentary ... voiceover has come to represent an authority and an aggressivity which can no longer be sustained"[22] in the wake of postmodern suspicion of the category of "truth." The ironic distance between what various narrators of Paizs's films describe and what the audience sees on screen bolsters this sense that such authority can no longer be sustained, even as many of Paizs's narrators overcompensate with increased aggressivity. In *Crime Wave*, the "claim to truth" that the documentary genre makes (a suspect claim but a claim nonetheless) invokes not confidence in the existence of some reality somewhere, but ironic undermining of the possibility of any access to reality or truth.

The End of Beginning

Steven's first ending to "Crime Wave" incorporates a crime movie staple, the car chase, during which Ronnie crashes into an already injured pedestrian and flies through the car's window to smash face-first into a telephone pole. We're treated to a comical silhouette of his splayed form, hanging above the ground, skull embedded in the pole from the force of the impact. Ronnie's limbs splay akimbo to suggest at once Wile E. Coyote and a crucified Jesus. Despite this bleak turn, the narrator announces that Ronnie, The King of tributes to The King, is "dead but not forgotten." This telephone pole has become a shrine to his memory. A small child attempts to stick his own face into the scar left in the wood by Ronnie's impact. The narrator chuckles and acknowledges that the boy can't quite fill Ronnie's shoes/face-impression now, but might one day. A macabre thought: the small boy might, if lucky and possessed by "a dream," manage to follow in Ronnie's murderous footsteps towards a violent death (to underscore this, Ronnie's "ghostly visage" appears over his "farewell impression" through a double exposure).[23] The narrator seems oblivious to this implication, and Steven, author of the narration, also seems oblivious. Thus, within five minutes, *Crime Wave* offers another hand-painted title card: "The End. A Steven Penny production." So much for the great Canadian epic.

What steps must Ronnie have taken to move from having "a dream" to "worldwide tribute domination"? How has Ronnie gone from his early failures to the heights of success, passing into immortality-as-icon? Without the middle, we don't know, and neither does Steven Penny. Herein lies his failure, as Kim returns to reveal: Steven has written many other beginnings and endings for "Crime Wave." He can only write beginnings and endings: "he has trouble with the stuff in-between." Steven (through Kim) reports that his failure results from perfectionism: "Steven wants to make 'Crime Wave' the best color crime movie there is, and to do that the script would have to be the best color crime script there is." This claim becomes suspicious, difficult to sustain as the film continues and we begin to suspect that the roots of Steven's inability to write middles go deeper, into the fundamental nature of his fantasy.

Crime Wave thus presents us with a beginning and ending that it then negates. What we have seen is not "Crime Wave" at all, but the failed results of an early draft – which nevertheless we have just viewed, produced by Paizs and cut into the final version of the film *Crime Wave*. The irony here – we are shown filmed scenes that the film then argues were never produced and do not exist – resolves itself later in the film, when Kim suggests that she has written a middle about Steven's struggle to write "Crime Wave" and thus rehabilitated Steven's failed scenes by reframing them within the current film (which nevertheless is not the film that Steven *wanted* to write: *Crime Wave* is not "Crime Wave"). The total effect is negation, although *Crime Wave*'s false starts continue to develop the story of Steven Penny himself.

In *The Book of Beginnings and Endings*, from which the epigraph to this book is taken, Jenny Boully presents the first and last pages of fictitious books, all of which are authored by "Jenny Boully" and titled "The Book of Beginnings and Endings." The middles are missing, but the subjects and typefaces reveal that these beginnings and endings do not even belong to the same volumes, despite other signals that they *are* all the same book (which they are, of course, on the literal level). Boully's book might be read as a Borgesian attempt to write not *a* book, but all of the *other* books one might have written instead. Paizs uses beginnings and endings in a far different manner. Steven Penny's production of beginnings and endings (which "are easy for him to think of") do not suggest a sublime proliferation of possible middles, but the impossibility of any middle – and, therefore, of completion. By extension, Steven's writings signal his inability to write. (Anyone who has ever written a book might sympathize, as the words pile up while the "book" itself seems to recede.) Paizs's unusual structure also calls to mind Jean-Luc Godard's comment that all films should have a beginning, middle, and end, though not necessarily in that order: Paizs plops his endings right after his beginnings, then negates them for new beginnings and endings, strewing shards of middles along the way (suggesting that no middle will ever cohere). Paizs's pastiche also calls to mind Godard's allusiveness: Peter Wollen writes that "as Godard's work developed, these quotations and allusions, instead of being a mark of eclecticism, began to take on an autonomy of their own ... Godard's own voice is drowned out and obliterated behind that of the authors quoted."[24] Paizs, by contrast, prefers to quote from and allude to paracinemas no filmgoer could expect to recognize in their particulars, that do not have authors/auteurs in the traditional sense, in a manner that does not obliterate but rather constructs a personal voice/style.

Crime Wave's bounty of beginnings and endings both obscures and underscores the absence of a "true" beginning and ending. In a way, the film is one big middle, into which we are thrown headlong. The plot twists to the point that we can't be sure what's happened and what's been dreamed (indeed, such distinctions are neither possible nor meaningful). When the film stops, even though we have just watched *Crime Wave*, Penny's dream of creating "Crime Wave" stands further afield. In its beginning, *Crime Wave* seems desperate to convince us that it will soon begin, but by its end the film has lost faith in the possibility of its own existence, that it might ever be begun.

A Portrait of Penny, Framed and Held Away

After foreshadowing the dangers that will assail Steven as a result of his having contracted this peculiar strain of writer's block (he "almost died twice" as a result), Kim brandishes a framed picture of Penny – his first appearance, in this picture frame, inside of a frame narrative. Steven is held at various removes throughout *Crime Wave*, with his silence as a "quiet man" serving as another distancing tactic. Throughout the film, we know that Steven speaks. People respond to him, although Paizs denies us shots of Steven speaking first. Kim also reports his speech, often in moments when, oddly, we see Steven's mouth move while Kim summarizes his dialogue. Paizs further distances the viewer from Steven visually, by framing him within frames for these first minutes. After the framed photo Kim presents, we next view Steven in two shots from Kim's point of view. First, we see Steven through the window of his apartment above the garage: in the crosshairs of the fourfold window frame, he steps motionless into view, all sagging shoulders and blank stares. Second, we see Steven again through this window, still in its crosshairs, dejected and gazing at the ground.

These moments when Steven is seen through the garage window mark one of Paizs's technical triumphs. Recalling the production, Paizs notes that "after a certain point I no longer had access to the house location, but I still needed all those POV shots featuring Steven in the garage. So I built a scale model of the side of the garage with the window, using ordinary materials like wood and cardboard and sandpaper (cut into little squares, the sandpaper looked like shingles on the roof)."[25] Paizs thus created a miniature of the garage and put himself in its window through in-camera special effects. This miniature "was about three feet high, but by positioning [myself] well back from it, like twenty or thirty feet back, I appeared, from the camera's POV, to be in scale to it ... All I needed to complete the illusion was to make sure I had enough depth of field to keep both the miniature and me in focus at the same time."[26] Such techniques recall the various methods Orson Welles used to achieve the sense of deep focus in *Citizen Kane*, and since *Crime Wave* will later "copy" *Kane* through an allusion in Steven's final ending to "Crime Wave," Paizs's technical reproduction of similar methods for perspective and focus are especially noteworthy. As well, in this garage miniature and thus in the finished film, the window where Steven Penny appears is framed by thick grey wood that mirrors the grey matte block enclosing Penny's photo in the frame Kim holds, so that the sense of Steven being "framed" is occurring within the film's *mise en scène* (his picture's in a frame, his body's framed in the garage window), on the narrative's structural level (via the frame of Kim's documentary reportage), and even during *Crime Wave*'s production process (as Paizs develops techniques to "frame" himself-as-Steven in the window of a miniature set).

We're also distanced from Steven through Kim's childlike inability to comprehend him. Kim tells us that "Steven was also a happy man," although we already have reason to suspect this, due to his unenthusiastic window appearances. Kim's explanation: "I could tell [he was happy] because on that first day I heard him laughing. He must have been a happy man because most people I know need the TV or a joke to make them laugh." Like the blithe statements of the narrator in the various beginnings and endings to "Crime Wave," Kim's narration, with its "explanation" of Steven, signals a missing of the mark. This ironic detachment works as another distancing tactic, presenting the opposite of the truth as indirect affirmation, pushing us from Penny even while relating information about him. (At the same time, this irony in a sense draws us closer to Paizs, through the sharing of a joke.) Paizs does treat us to Steven's laughter directly, the first of two rare moments that we hear him "speak" in the film's reality rather than in a fantasy scenario (both moments are expressions of pain: the first this unnerving, insane laughter, the second an "ouch" as he receives a needle). But by the time Kim climbs a tree to view him laughing (we've heard but not seen his cackling), he's already stopped.

What's the purpose of all this distancing? Why keep Steven at arm's length? On one hand, this distance serves to highlight Steven's failure, his inability to occupy the position he so craves: that of the Hollywood big shot, creator of the greatest color crime movie ever made. He's a big shot only in the eyes of Kim, an ignorant child with a schoolgirl crush.

Pevere has argued – in terms of Paizs's quiet man figure in general, from Billy to Nick to Steven – that he "can only be [construed] as heroic in a universe of his own making."[27] What we have in *Crime Wave*'s metafictional world is precisely this "quiet man" attempting to construct a universe of his own making, in which he might reign supreme. Steven's failure to write a satisfactory script for "Crime Wave" thus extends to his formal position in the film. He's incapable of properly being its protagonist and has to be dragged into the limelight by Kim. Even then, once onstage, he's unable to speak.

On the other hand, these distancing techniques also stand in defiance of the American film industry, in that they break the conventions of the Hollywood genres to which, in title and form, *Crime Wave* claims allegiance. Canadian cinema, when it comments on American cinema or on its own position in relation to that great beast, often adopts a critical, defensive, or passive-aggressive stance. By contrast, if we conflate Paizs and Penny in their ambition, *Crime Wave* seems to strike an aggressive pose. Paizs will do everything wrong, on purpose, and will *still* craft the greatest "color crime movie" ever made. (In its comic artistry, and as the only existing entry in this fictional genre, *Crime Wave* indeed wears the crown.) This brazenness, the unapologetic confidence that Paizs displays throughout *Crime Wave*, is apparent in even its smallest, most subtle moments (perhaps most strongly in these moments), yet it persists alongside admissions of self-doubt.

Kim tells us that Steven only writes by street light – but first, Paizs presents a darkened street lamp, which appears without explanation, in a silent close-up, after a jarring cut. This street light, in close-up at least, was created by Paizs using "one half of a bowling pin mould and a large plastic egg, both purchased at a crafts store [in] downtown [Winnipeg]."[28] In addition, "strips of vinyl carpet protector ... cut to fit"[29] provide interior texture. Such meticulous creation was typical of Paizs's approach to filmmaking and attests to both the symbolic import of the street light and Paizs's ability (on a tiny budget) to create homemade yet seamless effects (witness the aforementioned garage miniature, which Paizs created for "maybe a hundred dollars, maybe less").[30] Likewise, the night-time background is in fact "dark blue mat board with black airbrushing for trees."[31] Paizs's ability to create filmic illusion makes his occasional refusal to sustain the filmic illusion all the more significant. Similarly, his often-invisible editing, when it becomes noticeable, produces disorienting effects, as it does in this moment. Kim's contextualizing of this street light takes place after this extended shot, so that with the appearance of the street light it seems at first as if *Crime Wave* has stopped again and another movie taken its place. An orange glow builds within the lamp. The light flickers, fails, and then the lamp turns on with bright, loud humming.

This long, slow image of the flickering street light is repeated a number of times in the film. Each time the lamp takes longer and longer to flicker to life – and since Steven waits until the street lights come on before tapping his typewriter keys, the prospect that the lamp might fail gets tangled with the prospect of Steven's own failure. As one reviewer notes: "Never has the switching on of a simple street light seemed so fraught with longing and dread."[32] The recurrent motif of struggling street lights is a poetic image (connected, as in the poetic epigraph of this book, to beginnings and endings, turning on as the night begins and day ends). Since Steven writes in the light of this lamp, we can view its progressive difficulty turning on as a metaphor for his progressive difficulty with the script. When Steven does write his final beginning and ending to "Crime Wave," it is only after a similar street lamp falls, shattering, and enfolds his head, which is then lit by the supernatural glow of his new ideas (a clear development of this symbolism).

The morning after Steven's first night of writing, Kim awakens to a bright, jaunty score. She spies Steven delivering the crumpled pages of his night's writings to the trash cans behind Kim's garage. This is our first non-framed shot of Steven – in his failure – although we still see him in long establishing shots, from Kim's point of view. Later, while playing with a ball outside, Kim investigates Steven's trashed script pages. As she reads, we're treated to disparate scenes from his abandoned middles. Ronnie Boyles is involved in a hunting accident, gets a cancer diagnosis, and has run his lawn mower over a child's pet hamster. Nothing seems to connect these scenes, and it is not clear how they would lead Ronnie to either superstardom or downfall. Precisely the point, of course, and why Steven has rejected these "middles." As the mailman comes whistling to deliver Steven's mail, another metafictional wrinkle might pass unnoticed. This mailman, in the film's diegesis, whistles the extra-diegetic tune that played on the film's soundtrack moments ago. This tune returns again and again throughout *Crime Wave*, as an element in Paizs's pastiche, a conscious evocation of American sitcom soundtracks.[33] The recycling of this tune further unsettles the narrative status of the on-screen events, as if the mailman had been watching the film and gotten the catchy tune stuck in his head before stepping into frame. Paizs's pastiche does not limit itself to copying the surfaces of other films, or copying elements (such as the "quiet man") from his own other films. He even copies structures (the multiple beginnings and endings) and elements (in this case, the musical score) from within the film itself. In this way, his pastiche aesthetic, as expressed within *Crime Wave*, marries itself to the metafictional structure with winking nods to filmic artifice.

Another aural joke plays out as Steven comes downstairs to get the mail. Kim flees into some nearby bushes, script pages in hand, afraid to be discovered with her nose in Steven's business. Steven decides to discard the day's mail. As Kim watches from the bushes, dramatic music begins with Steven's perusal of the mail, builds during his walk, reaches a crescendo as he opens the trash can lid to discover his script pages are gone – and then dies as he drops the junk mail in and lowers the lid

Dave Peter and Shawn Wilson (both also responsible for special make-up and effects), as Ronnie Boyles's hunting buddies. Courtesy of John Paizs, from the director's personal collection.

without reacting (Steven's inexpressive face almost never reacts). Steven *has* noticed, however, as Kim discovers. She decides to save all of his discarded drafts, shoving them under her rug (later on she complains that her rugs are becoming lumpy as Steven continues to produce unworkable middles). When she heads out in the rain the next day to save Steven's night's work, she finds it wrapped in plastic on top of the trashcan, presented with a yellow ribbon. Steven stands off to the side, regarding her from underneath an umbrella. This our first medium shot of Steven, as we finally come "closer" to him – as does Kim, who announces that they are now best friends.

Persistence of Vision

What else would fast friends do but explain to each other the phenomenon of persistence of vision? Steven draws the chalk outline of a splayed body in marker on a piece of paper, complete with bloody wound (but instead of red for the blood, Steven uses a festive green marker). He adds a black bullet hole in the centre of the wound, in keeping with Penny's taste for color crime movies. Kim passes on Steven's instruction that she stare at the black dot in the drawing for "two choruses of 'When the Saints Come Marching In,'" which Steven will play on his harmonica. Then, Steven will turn the sheet over to reveal a new page, blank except for a single black dot in the same position. Kim will stare at that dot until she sees the body. Kim encourages the spectator to join in on the fun: "C'mon, you try it too! Remember, keep your eyes only on the black dots."

In his analysis of this scene, Cagle draws attention to Kim's address of "the spectator, who may or may not experience the phenomenon explained in the previous moments, [and who] is left sitting in the dark and staring at a (nearly) blank screen. The narrative grinds to a halt … as the viewer is left to ponder a dark spot on a white field … the heretofore invisible processes, both technical and intertextual, by which the 'magic' of movies is achieved are thus exposed by means of a magnificently simple gesture."[34] The straightforwardness of this gesture prevents true disjunction: although the narrative may "grind to a halt," it is not overthrown, only suspended. Paizs's commitment to entertainment separates *Crime Wave*'s postmodernism from the more radical gestures of experimental film, yet the seeming simplicity of *Crime Wave* masks its dark, subversive core. Kim next explains (with the aid of further hand-drawn diagrams) what persistence of vision is and how it makes movie watching possible. "Did you know," she asks, "that since it takes the projector more time to move between frames than to project them, we're actually looking at a blank screen for longer than anything?" Her father, a bit baffled by the sudden science lesson (as is, perhaps, the film's audience), jokes that the next time he goes to the movies, he'll "have to demand cut-rate." The awkward exchange and the diagrammatic explanations give the sequence the feel of a grade school educational film, with Paizs copying inept paracinema techniques. This light-hearted, silly bit of audience engagement demystifies and draws attention to the filmic processes involved, in a gesture of postmodern self-reflexivity. However, violence and despair pervade even otherwise light moments of *Crime Wave*, and we can see Kim's explanation of the "black screen" as a metaphor for this dark undercurrent.

The perverse suggestion throughout *Crime Wave* is that, on the metafictional level where *Crime Wave* and "Crime Wave" intersect, the film represents not the culmination and success of Steven's dream but its absolute death. The viewer is watching, simultaneously, both a light-hearted, "Totalcolor" realization of Steven's filmic quest and a black screen shrouding his ambitions (which persists just a little longer). This interpretation makes more sense by the film's conclusion, when we're treated to Steven's final beginning and ending, where his failure has become the ironic subject (the implicit message beneath explicit praise of his wild success). We next see Kim gaze wistfully at a scrap of blank paper. She imagines Steven's body there, splayed out like the figure he has drawn to explain the optical illusion. This kind of daydreaming naturally results from Kim's schoolgirl crush, but we mustn't fail to realize, even if Kim cannot, that Steven's body, by appearing in her daydreams this way, "fills in" the chalk outline he's drawn, like a corpse.

This connection between the "persistence of vision" outline that Steven draws and Steven's own bodily death is emphasized in one version of Paizs's script. After deciding to reshoot the ending, Paizs wrote a new ending that, unlike the film's original ending (discussed in chapter 7), presents Steven's "final" beginning and ending to "Crime Wave." Many differences persist between this rewritten version and the reshot ending of the finished film, and some of these (like other alterations from Paizs's early scripts) are of interest insofar as they extend the themes of the finished film. In the final version of the film, Steven's corpse (in his "ending" fantasy) is cryogenically frozen. In the script, Steven's corpse is "preserved for the ages in a glass-covered coffin" where "his arms are outstretched in the 'persistence of vision' pose."[35] As the mourners exit Steven's tomb, they see "a double exposure of Steven in the 'persistence' pose [on] sidewalks, buses, and billboards."[36] The script thus returns, in this planned ending, to both the phenomenon of persistence of vision and the pose Steven drew in explanation. The image of Steven's posed corpse "persists" in the viewer's vision, bleeding into the next shot through the double exposure. In the finished film, of course, which lacks this scene, Steven's "persistence" operates on another level: my interpretation insists on "seeing" Penny's corpse overlaid everywhere in this final declaration of triumph, while others may accept without irony Kim's insistence that she and Steven will shoot to the heights of color crime movie stardom through their own persistence.

Paizs's screenplay for *Crime Wave* is worth discussing in more detail here, since the "persistence of vision" sequence is absent from the original script (in both its handwritten and typed versions). Steven shows Kim "these things called squibs that were used to make pretend gun shot holes."[37] The sequence remains playful but contains a dark suggestiveness. To begin with, the "special balloon" that Steven uses to hold the fake blood is "a condom."[38] Although Kim does not know this (Paizs reveals it in a footnote), and the scene appears innocent, we still have a grown man and a young girl playing together with a condom. The script also suggests political undertones to the play violence: "to make it more fun, [Kim and Steven] pretended that [Kim] was a policeman and Steven was a communist" and then later that they "were both from Ireland."[39] However playful this scene, their role playing connects Steven's fantasy violence to real-world political violence. Steven makes Kim complicit in this violence: she pretends to shoot him, and his gut and back explode. Later on, while in church, Kim daydreams "that squibs are going off on the priest, altar boys and members of the choir."[40] Most disturbing, after demonstrating squibs, Steven shows Kim his "special knives that made pretend cuts."[41] While doing so, he "draws the knife across her throat, leaving a pretend blood slit."[42] In the blackest scene in *Crime Wave*'s script (absent, as noted above, from the finished film), Kim then hears her father outside and "runs to the window." Mr Brown does a "delayed take on [her] cut throat."[43] Kim does not understand his concern and is overjoyed at Steven's promises "to show [her] more later."[44] Although these scenes are cut from the film and replaced with the "persistence of vision" sequence, the film nevertheless continues to develop this undercurrent of violence.

Pump Up the Violence

In his second beginning and ending, Steven attempts to solve his story problems as Hollywood would, by cranking up the violence and cutting back on character motivations. This time, the "racket" is Allway product direct distribution (an Amway-esque direct marketing scheme), and our heroes "from the North" are a couple, Skip and Dawn Holliday. They escalate to violence more quickly than Ronnie. Skip displays strawberry aerosol spray to a near-catatonic home audience, while Dawn is off in the "little girl's room." Actually, Dawn is away stealing from the family's bedroom. When caught in the act by an elderly relation of the customers, Dawn yells out. Skip then murders the husband, crushing his skull with a glass ashtray, and chases the fleeing, wheelchair-bound wife into the kitchen. He shoves a broom between the spokes of her wheelchair and, with murderous glee, begins stuffing her mouth with dog biscuits. (The bizarre visual prominence of the bag of dog biscuits seems to anticipate the now-pervasive practice of product placement in films. That manner of force-feeding advertising to a movie audience is here presented as a literal force-feeding.) "And so," trumpets our exuberant narrator, while they soap the dead hands to slip off the jewellery of their victims, "Skip and Dawn Holliday take their first fateful steps on the road to worldwide direct distributors domination!"

The violence in this second beginning is more brutal and less motivated than in Steven's previous beginning, and it escalates more quickly. Steven's new ending is also both more schmaltzy and more vicious. At an Allway awards show, Skip and Dawn are called up to receive lapel pins recognizing them as "triple-diamond record breakers!" In a heartfelt speech, Skip notes: "It's only in a great country like this that all that's happened to us happened to a couple like us." Skip goes on to make the standard clichéd statements that in other nations social mobility is less possible, hard work bears fewer rewards, and so forth, with direct reference to the "bamboo or iron curtain." Skip doesn't name this "great country" but it is clear from his attitude which country he means. The Canadian Steven has set his tale down south.

The notion that violence is a typically American problem, a typically American solution to problems, and a typically American subject – or pleasure – is ingrained in the Canadian imagination and recurs throughout Canadian cinema. In an analysis of *A History of Violence* (2005), Bart Beaty notes that David Cronenberg's film presents the "premise that violence is fundamental to American middle-class life, and that it exists in every aspect of that life."[45] A similar premise is implicit in and fundamental to *Crime Wave*. Its presence here is of a different tenor, and Paizs seems concerned not with the violence *of* middle-class life but rather with the violence *enjoyed by* the middle-class – a national, cultural, filmic obsession with crime. We next get what we expect (and perhaps desire) as audience to a crime film: Skip's speech is interrupted by the police, who arrive to arrest the duo and without provocation blow out Skip's chest with a shotgun blast. Dawn cries out, bending over Skip, but her concern is not for him but for his new lapel pin, which she steals before running away. In Paizs's scripts, the Holliday scenes are even more violent. Instead of "just" murdering her, Skip begins to rape the wheelchair-bound woman.[46] The Holliday death scenes are also more brutal: in the original handwritten script, "Skip's head is blown clear off" and "the officers open up on [Dawn] and reduce her to pulp."[47] Paizs's various scripts show that, in production, he consistently made efforts to lighten the tone and downplay the violence. He did not exorcise it, however, and in its repression it bears more power. One might even view Paizs's light-hearted treatment of violence as more subversive, since it rejects an easy position of critique, complicating and troubling the position of the viewer and the stance of the characters in relation to *Crime Wave*'s comic brutality.

Skip has internalized American capitalist ideology at its most schizophrenic: the pursuit of the "American Dream" is both a vicious competition with one's fellows and a common striving that unifies the nation. Dawn internalizes the tangible rewards of this way of thinking, possessive to the end: she flees after Skip is shot, but another officer blows off her foot, and she collapses – then swallows the lapel pins. The development from the "tribute racket" to the "direct distributor racket" also signals a shift from artistic competition to capitalist competition, as Penny moves further towards the blatant equation of success with gain that his narrator will draw in the final beginning and ending to "Crime Wave."

As the corpses of Skip and Dawn are autopsied, waxen faces pale beneath morgue lights, the narrator proclaims their strange immortality: "The Hollidays are dead. But the mark of their achievement would live on, a shining beacon beckoning those couples who, like Skip or Dawn, had a dream." It's significant that, once again, this dream is not questioned, and Steven seems blind to the fact that the "dream," both for Ronnie Boyles and for Skip and Dawn Holliday, begins in murder and ends in death. It's also notable that the chase sequence of Dawn's failed escape mirrors Ronnie's car chase from the previous ending to "Crime Wave." Steven has already fallen into formulae, reproducing in his second script a disguised version of his first, which foreshadows his eventual dissatisfaction with the scenario even as the film offers it to the viewer – another narrative negation.

The (Further) Education of Kim

Kim's excitement at a new beginning and ending to "Crime Wave" falters as Steven renews his habit of trashing his middles. She takes them to school to read, and we're again treated to disassociated moments. Skip ties Dawn to the bed while making banal comments that neckties are an improvement over the extension cords that have been biting into her ankles. As he does so, Skip whistles the same tune that Dr Jolly will later whistle, in another postmodern undermining of the distinction between narrative levels (this is supposed to be Steven's script, while Jolly later appears in "reality"). In another middle, Skip opens his car door in the midst of a traffic jam to injure a bicyclist for the couple's amusement. The cars in this traffic jam were actually arranged in a parking lot in the St Boniface neighbourhood of Winnipeg, but Paizs "stole" a shot of an actual traffic jam from downtown Winnipeg to introduce the short scene. That single shot, Paizs notes, "sells the rest of it"[48] (through tricks like this Paizs managed to keep within his modest budget). Kim's schoolroom features an easy-to-miss joke: the blackboard behind Kim's teacher (played by Kovacs's older sister) bears two questions for the kids:

1. *Should you believe everything you hear?*
2. *Should you believe everything you read?*

These throwaway jokes prefigure both Bart Simpson's blackboard scribbling and the background jokes that *The Simpsons* would later popularize. *Simpsons*-esque, "freeze-frame" jokes became common in the age of the videocassette – fitting, then, that *Crime Wave*'s only significant release was to VHS. Paizs, commenting on this phenomenon, says that "I see a lot of what I was doing in shows like *The Simpsons* or *Family Guy* ... sudden cutaways to something that relates to something that was just said."[49]

Steven continues his education of Kim, showing her his Bolex 16mm camera and his favourite film stock, Kodak-Eastman 7291. Together, they watch the magical blue sparkle (which Paizs produced through a double exposure) as the film is first unboxed.[50] The Bolex that Steven displays is the same camera Paizs used to shoot much of *Crime Wave* (of course, for this scene, he used another camera, the Winnipeg Film Group's Arriflex).[51] This film stock was also used to shoot *Crime Wave*. For a few night scenes, Paizs used a faster-speed film, but he found it too grainy and reshot most of those scenes.[52] (Ironically, the stock wasn't sensitive enough to capture its own real-world sparkle, necessitating the special effect.[53])

Does Paizs, in these moments, slip out of Steven's character and start playing himself? If so, we might read the next moment with more pathos: all is not smiles and blue sparkles. As Penny returns the film stock to his refrigerator, he stops suddenly to stare into it for a long time – the music stops as well, the film grinding to another halt. It's an odd moment, one that jars the viewer, but once Penny begins moving again, Kim explains: "That was one of Steven's attacks of self-doubt." In the original script, Kim expands by adding that these attacks of self-doubt "don't really have anything to do with how movies are made, but, for Steven had a lot to do with making movies."[54] That *Crime Wave* takes itself as its subject makes the inscription, within the film, of self-doubt concerning the importance of this subject all the more poignant.

Steven also plays Kim a sound recording of the time a car accident destroyed the camera he'd borrowed from the National Film Board, almost killing him and costing him $2,000. Later on, when the movie he had been filming was released, "almost nobody liked it." Her parents tsk over the photos of the accident Kim shows them:

MRS BROWN: Steven should have maybe had some professional help.
MR BROWN: You spend a small fortune and you could lose your shirt. And what's to keep him from making another dud?

Here Paizs has transmuted another personal moment into the stuff of his film's fantasy. While filming *Springtime in Greenland*, the driver of Corny Blower's car lost control as he raced towards the camera, almost hitting Paizs and clipping the tripod so that the camera he had rented from the National Film Board smashed into the pavement. Paizs reports that "those pictures of the accident that Kim is showing her parents at the dinner table ... are the real thing, taken after the police arrived on scene."[55] The audio recording that Steven plays Kim, of the crash,

Steven Penny (John Paizs) has an attack of self-doubt. Courtesy of John Paizs, from the director's personal collection.

is also authentic.[56] (However, *Springtime* was well received, in contrast to Steven's unnamed film.) As in the "persistence of vision" scene, by laying bare the material processes of cinema production, Paizs again demystifies the physical supports of the filmic illusion. Later, in Steven Penny's final scripted ending, a similar undercutting occurs, this time of Steven's own fantasy (dismantling its possibility rather than showcasing its methods).

Kim's parents stand in for Steven's own, who are absent throughout the film, although we can assume their disapproval given that Steven has been reduced to renting a garage attic. We learn nothing about Steven's personal life and can conclude that he doesn't have one. He appears to be without friends (aside from the young Kim, an unusual and perhaps inappropriate friendship), and he has no love life, only a single-minded obsession with crafting the perfect "Crime Wave" script. Steven Penny is a Kafkan character, in Milan Kundera's sense that Kafka's characters are not "unique being[s]" in that they have no backstory (Kafka's K. has neither a "proper" name nor any personal history in the conventional sense) and their "field[s] of action [are] lamentably limited" since they are "absorbed by the situation [they find themselves] trapped in."[57] Steven certainly seems trapped in the world of *Crime Wave*'s metafiction, in that all of his attempts to pursue his goals bring him both no closer to those goals and deeper into the film, as Steven goes from being the writer to becoming the protagonist of his own script.

By now the comic potential of *Crime Wave*'s structure, which can accommodate any joke in the flexible edifice of its unstable diegesis, is clear. We can understand why Bruce McCulloch, after seeing the film on late night television, hired Paizs to direct for *The Kids in the Hall* – Paizs to some degree had anticipated the tone, style, and structure of their absurdist skits. Paizs uses this unstable structure as a container for a hodgepodge of genre content, marginal film styles, and film-within-a-film sketches, winding everything into the overall narrative of Steven's attempts to craft "Crime Wave." This is why, for all of its gathering of disparate styles and tropes, there is a startling coherence to Paizs's film and vision. *Crime Wave*'s structure can subsume any elements so that, however bizarre their juxtaposition, they appear to belong together. Maddin's films have been both praised and criticized for the way his pastiche of film styles prevents the viewer from engaging with his narrative – for sacrificing plot to psychodrama and emotionally charged, melodramatic excess. By contrast, in Paizs's films, the audience is disengaged from the emotional lives of characters; yet despite occasionally absurd developments the plot remains clear, with narrative engagement a given.

Snakes and Ladders

As the story advances, and Steven's writer's block worsens, Kim's carpet grows lumpier with his discarded middles. She hears less and less typing at night. Kim tries to distract Steven from his troubles by taking him on walks and with an odd but well-meant plan: "Hey! I have an idea! I could sneak you in later, and when my Dad gets back from the club, we can listen to my Mom and Dad do it. They always do it after that." This bizarre invitation might inject a disturbing sexual tension into Steven and Kim's relationship, if Kim didn't seem so innocent in the moment of its utterance, and if Steven didn't fail to react. As it stands, he thanks Kim for the offer but declines as if she'd offered him a cashew. He trudges upstairs to await nightfall. The street light takes even longer to flicker on, and its light frames Steven in the garage window with his hands not on the keys but covering his face. After a long pause, we see that Kim is awake, standing in her darkened bedroom, staring out of the window towards Steven. Then we hear slow, erratic typing. Steven starts over for the third time, crafting another beginning and ending for "Crime Wave."

This third beginning follows Steven's established formula, which bodes ill. Steven's subject this time is the self-help racket, with competing gurus promoting various buzzwords. In Paizs's scripts, alternative "rackets" abound, including an "animal ad racket" and an "answers racket"[58] that both suggest the formulaic nature of Steven's imagination in their interchangeability. The hero of this new "Crime Wave," the young Stanley Falco, reads something in his kitchen (a self-help article he's written, no doubt). Falco grunts in frustration and throws the pages to the ground, stomping on them and then scrabbling to his knees to tear them apart. Although we have seen Steven's ambitions reflected in his previous characters, now we instead see his frustrations transcribed: Stanley, like Steven, is dissatisfied with something he's written. Face contorting as if possessed (perhaps by Steven, who seems here to be self-punishing in Stanley's guise), he brushes the floor clear and begins to smash his head against it. In the "answers racket" script version of this scene, Steven's indecision about how to develop the plot of "Crime Wave" is more directly copied onto Stanley's predicament. On a busy street, Stanley "stares up at a brick wall that has two arrows painted on it. He can't choose whether to follow one or the other. He begins to brutally beat his head against the wall."[59]

And so, the blithe narrator proclaims, "Stanley Falco took his first fateful steps on the road to worldwide self-help domination." For the first time, Steven-as-author seems aware of the ironic distance between what his narrator says and what we see. Despite what he might think, Steven is moving closer to his fantasy, not further from it, and as he draws closer this gap is more apparent. Although this beginning is otherwise formulaic, the violence here is self-directed, of a different order than the violence of Ronnie or the Hollidays. The ending to this new version of "Crime Wave" breaks with tradition as well. It continues only a few moments after its beginning, the "middle" action clear. Stanley still pounds his head on the kitchen floor. By now a pool of blood stains the flooring tile, which is patterned with snakes and ladders that suggest Stanley's (and Steven's) inability to progress towards his dream, caught as he is in the up-and-down movement of producing ideas he must discard.

4

The Stuff In-Between

Steven is too deep in despair to even throw his new beginning and ending in the garbage, and Kim takes this lack of morning trash as a positive sign. She fantasizes about Steven's stunning success, which in her childish world means that he would still live above her garage and let her display him at "show and tell." The blackboard in her dreamed scene captures Kim's childlike naivety: Steven stands before the class as Kim lectures, pointing to him with a metre stick, while in the background Kim has chalked a smiling stick-figure Steven in the "persistence of vision" pose. Paizs thus presents Kim's distorted gaze within the fantasy space, where the disjuncture between her view and ours is comedic (the chalk outline Steven drew has been turned into a chalk figure, the corpse smiling now, happy to play its part in a color crime movie).

Kim's appropriation of the image effectively empties out the violence of the "persistence" pose, which by now has been transformed and "made safe" through its repetition. Kim's proximity to *Crime Wave*'s imagery has this repressive tendency to strip otherwise violent or sexual content of its edge, which is one reason why the film takes a darker turn in its later acts, as Steven leaves for Kansas without Kim. Kim's retreat from the narrative occasions its unmooring from reality and its development in nightmarish directions, in terms of both plot events and production design. Kim helps sustain Steven's fantasy (she views him with awe, as the success he imagines he might be), so distance from her brings Steven closer to the fantasy's dissolution, to traumatic encounter with the "real," which is revealed in the breaking apart of his final typewritten words.

Kim soon realizes "the awful truth" of Steven's failure, and hysterically reports his new plan, which is "to not eat or drink and let his beard and fingernails and toenails grow and stare at the ceiling until he starved!" Her father, less concerned, replies, "That's his privilege and I suggest you don't bother him so much." Seeing that only she can save Steven, Kim leaves food for him, but it remains untouched. She unlocks his door with a spare key and shoves the dinner inside. Steven's garage apartment has its door set on a slant, "to hide the fact that there is no stairwell beneath the door" in the later shots where Kim enters Steven's apartment.[1] Since the set was built at the University of Manitoba and neither "raising the set [n]or cutting into the actual floor" was an option, "Eva needed to crouch beneath the door before opening it and stepping through."[2] In this shot, she does neither: instead, she's seen from outside, and just opens the door a crack to slide in food and later to see that it's been nibbled on. But Steven has no newfound appetite; his apartment has rats.

Exterminators break in, to the bizarre sight of Steven, shirtless on the bed, allowing rats to eat him. This, perhaps, is the moment that most confirms Paizs's personal dedication: he recalls putting "peanut butter on my arm to get the rat to gnaw on it."[3] His intention was to use this shot of the rats eating Penny "to bring that first half of the sequence to a peak. I was very meticulous about the way I went about everything in the film. Very conscious of its rise and fall as we move through the sequences. Shot it ... jigsaw puzzle style, every beat pre-visualized and storyboarded accordingly. Almost nothing left to chance. Though the rat-gnawing-arm moment might very well qualify as one of our 'what were we thinking' ones, in how we went about getting it."[4]

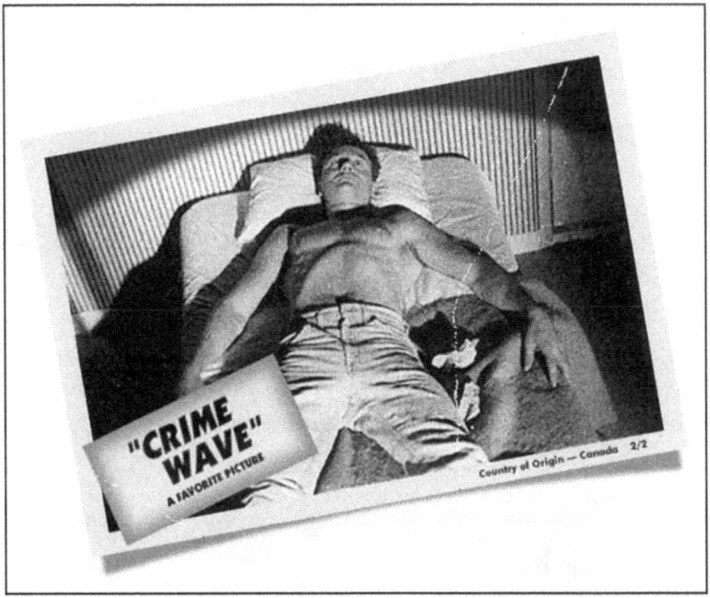

Promotional photo card from *Crime Wave*, in which Steven Penny (John Paizs) has given up hope and is waiting for rats to eat him. Courtesy of John Paizs, from the director's personal collection.

Steven gasps audibly as he takes a buttock injection, an expression of pain we might regard as especially existential given his lack of speech elsewhere. Although Steven seems to perk up after this experience – he dines with the family, agrees to go to a costume party, and joins them for snacks and late night television – it becomes clear that his strange, suicidal depression is only a precursor to something far worse. Kim fears that although Steven seems better on the outside, inside he has given up on color crime movies, and even suicide-by-rat, and that he may be considering "getting a real job" – an ironic suggestion that writing color crime movies isn't "a real job," but Steven's way to avoid joining society and taking up his designated space among the working class. Steven plans to vault from his dropout position as a starving artist to soar above the crowd as a movie mogul. His dreams of wild success thereby introduce a further irony: his capitalistic entrepreneurship as an independent filmmaker is also his excuse to avoid assuming his proper "role" within the capitalist structure. His fantasy allows him to preserve his self-identity as a struggling artist while enjoying the perks of success. In his final ending scenario, Steven envisions achieving just such a blend of artistic and commercial success.

The "Giving Up" Party

Steven's already suspected status as a social isolate is confirmed in the costume party scenes: he shows up dressed as "Nelson Mingus," who (according to Kim) tried to rob a Royal Bank the previous year. Steven's costume consists of fake dynamite, duct-taped to his bare chest, and a look of utter insanity. He's greeted by the other partygoers with nervous, shrill laughter. Whenever he sidles up to a chattering group, its members flee, surreptitiously at first but soon looking him in the face and turning to run. Dejected, Steven leans himself against the kitchen appliances, only to be greeted by a sultry, black-hatted seductress. In the script she is named "Cherry" and described as "a drunk, sluttish Joan Collins type,"[5] but in the film she has no name, only a question: "What are you waiting for?" She seems like a fantasy woman akin to "Connie" from *The Obsession of Billy Botski*, but with the flair of a degraded femme fatale. After Kim collects Steven from the bathroom where he has been taken by this temptress, the toilet flushes as they walk away down the hall. Kim seems confused (how could Steven flush the toilet when he's no longer in the bathroom?), and Steven feigns innocence. Although this femme fatale does not develop her narrative potential, this is perhaps the point: Steven, faced with a real-life figure from the kind of crime movie he hopes to write, can't sustain or deepen the relationship. Neither as author nor as protagonist can he take the film where it wants to go – a harbinger of how his final approach to writing "Crime Wave," and his attempts to take hold of his fantasy, will play out.

Soon after, Steven and Kim leave the party on an errand, and become transfixed by a sight in another guest's parked car. A sexual scene: they glimpse a woman's naked back in the act of arching over and down. She looks like the woman who seduced Steven earlier at the party. Kim is confused, and Steven's face remains inscrutable as ever. The film's strange sexual undercurrent arises again – these sexual moments are not "consummated," in the sense that they seem to go nowhere. They are senseless testaments to a desire that neither Steven nor his ailing film can direct fruitfully. Thus, they are in keeping with *Crime Wave*'s overall theme of errant perversity, and the presence of inappropriate desire permeates the film. Such moments also attest to Steven's sense that something or someone has stolen his enjoyment (to use the Lacanian formulation that grounds paranoiac fantasy), although Steven has yet to determine who or what. It is implied that Steven and "Cherry" had sex in the bathroom, but when Steven views the woman's naked back in this other car it seems as if he's forgotten his recent conquest and that he desires with wistful longing an "impossible" event that has already occurred. When Steven seats himself alongside Kim, a preteen girl whose company he cannot enjoy sexually, it emphasizes the difference between what's happening in this car (his actual life) and what's happening in the other (a fantasy scenario). That Steven seems here to long hopelessly for the very woman he has just "enjoyed" undercuts the possibility that he might be able to actually enjoy any such fantasy realizations. In the psychoanalytic situation, this inability to enjoy might be focused on some Other, whom the subject's fantasy designates as the cause of that inability: if not for the Other, the subject could enjoy fully. However, as Steven's bathroom sex made clear, Steven operates as his own Other: he is the one who cannot write middles, he is the one who cannot enjoy. His fantasy might hold this realization at bay, but over the course of the film he comes closer and closer to it. The inkling of this realization is established here, and fully assumed later in the film when Steven writes himself into his script (viewing himself as the "Other" explicitly, taking an "outside" position in relation to himself and his fantasy).

The Boundless Horror of "A Real Job"

Before they leave the party and see "Cherry" in the other car, Kim introduces Steven to another "quiet man" named Lyle, the son of the party hosts. Although Lyle's interests ("planets and dinosaurs") align with those of boys Kim's own age, Lyle appears older than Steven (a vision of his possible future, perhaps). Lyle is misanthropic: he complains that "the average size of a dinosaur's brain was no bigger than a walnut, but at least they used most of it," and while the partygoers perform the "chicken dance" downstairs Lyle disillusions Kim by telling her that astronomy reveals that "Jesus was probably born years before most people say and not on Christmas at all." Steven, through his professional ambitions, wants to set himself apart from others, but in his professional failure this setting apart turns him into an isolate. He's a social failure as well as a professional one, a misfit like Lyle: Steven just lives with Kim's parents, whereas Lyle lives with his own. In his passivity and failure, Steven is a typically Canadian protagonist, despite his distinctly American ambitions. *Crime Wave*, for all of its uniqueness, shares what Pevere calls "that most careworn of Canadian narrative concerns: the individual chronically alienated from society ... what may rank as the predominant thematic tradition in English-Canadian movies."[6] Where Paizs's film differs is in revealing this "narrative concern" as a Canadian fantasy: a paranoiac assumption that Canada's proximity to the United States has resulted in social alienation, producing the nation's fabled passivity.

Lyle's mother sends the trio on an errand (she says that the party needs more mix, but maybe she just wants to get rid of them for a while), and since Steven is considering "a real job," Lyle presents him with one possible option. On their way to the convenience store, he stops to explain that he works as a car counter for the City of Winnipeg's traffic department. Paizs himself worked a similar job as a traffic clerk in Winnipeg, while producing *Crime Wave* and many of his short films. Lyle and Steven are both connected to Paizs through their jobs (traffic clerk and filmmaker), which cements their interconnection. As part of his job, Lyle must note how many cars approach the intersection and how they turn, so that traffic lights can be properly set and timed. As Lyle performs this task, Paizs injects the night-time scene with false drama. In a long series of shots, Lyle hesitates over a car that appears to be turning right, but then feints left before finally turning right, so that Lyle almost counts the car wrong although he ultimately succeeds. Sweat beads on his brow – but what would counting the car wrong matter? Kim exaggerates the importance of the job, presumably because Lyle also does: "sometimes people were late for work or even died because the lights were set wrong." Kim thus presents Lyle's delusion to us in a way that makes its delusional qualities apparent. This is a fantasy of meaningful work, similar to Steven's exaggerations about the cultural power of "color crime movies." Lyle goes on to explain that the "best part of the job was the other guys." As Kim reports this speech, the camera holds steady on Lyle, alone and unmoving, staring straight ahead into the darkness. What "other guys"? Kim takes what he says at face value and is easily impressed – she gapes at Lyle's "banana stickers from all over the world," just as she's awed by Steven's claim to be a color crime movie maker. Kim also takes note of Lyle's "postcard from an ex-car-counter who won the lottery and moved to Florida." We can see that the postcard has been torn in half and taped back together. Lyle is less happy in his job than Kim believes, and buys his own lottery ticket once they reach the convenience store (in service to another fantasy, of impossible escape).

Lyle seems pathetic, both in his isolation and in needing Kim to "speak" for him (another "quiet man"), and as such, he is an unattractive embodiment of Steven's possible future in "a real job." The "Lyle" sequence ends with Steven's inexpressive face. Now that the nightmarish world of "real jobs" has been revealed, he spends the next few weeks not job-hunting but biking around aimlessly and "looking at things." These "things" provide him with little inspiration. He reports to Kim "a place where the streetcars used to go," in acknowledgment of the city's better days, when the rails thrived and Winnipeg boomed – poised, perhaps, to develop into a thriving filmmaking mecca instead of giving birth to the depressed industry that Steven inherits (a variation on the eternal Winnipeg fantasy of "what might have been"). Steven also notes "two puddles that never seemed to dry," in ironic contrast to his own dried-up wells of inspiration.

Steven's most exciting discovery is a traffic accident where the jaws of life must be deployed. His reaction to the scene is disturbing and revealing. He perches on his bicycle as a callous spectator, snacking as he would while watching a color crime movie. Here is some real-world violence – a destroyed car, a bloodied crash victim – but the real-world rescue lacks the drama and excitement of Steven's own imagined car accident (the one that sends Ronnie Boyles flying through the windshield into a telephone pole). Steven thus feels the need to insert drama: he worries that "if they weren't careful, [the jaws of life] might fall into the wrong hands." What he imagines a criminal mastermind might do with the jaws of life Kim does not say: since he is no longer writing "Crime Wave," Steven has no outlet for his imaginative energies. Steven's fascination with violence and his own troubling relationship to that fascination – snacking while he watches the victim bleed – develops the film's critical stance towards its protagonist, which will blossom into Steven's self-critical stance later on, when narrative levels collapse in the final beginning and ending to "Crime Wave."

Steven's writer's block spurs a sense of mounting danger. Having been confirmed, through his interaction with Lyle, as a misfit and an isolate, he begins to hang out with other social misfits (effeminate punk-styled men) in the afternoon, loitering on the sidewalk. In Paizs's script, Kim refers to Steven's inclusion in a club of sorts: "all you had to do to be in the club was as little as possible."[7] The sense that Steven, through his self-imposed isolation, is joining an ironic "club" of isolates or otherwise becoming part of some subculture, is lacking from the finished film, with the effect that there seems nothing heroic or idealistic about Steven's withdrawal. Kim does not perceive his isolation: "It was a good life," she reports, "but sometimes guys in half-ton trucks wanted to speak to them." These truckers, whom the credits term "hillbillies," are an element carried over (copied) to *Crime Wave* from *The International Style*, and reappear again and again throughout *Crime Wave* to represent the growing threat of Steven's creative deprivation. Perhaps he fears that his lack of imagination puts him in the same league as these truck-driving hillbillies. At the very least it puts Steven in danger of harassment by a social order that neither values his creativity nor sympathizes with his lack thereof: "Get a job, homo," the hillbillies yell to one skateboarder after beaning him with a pear.

The "Crime Wave" Club

At night, when he should be writing, Steven's failures return to haunt him, in the form of a depressing social club peopled by characters from the different versions of "Crime Wave." Kim tells us that "Steven was the only real person in [this club] ... They all mainly sat around and thought of what might have been." In the original version of the script, the characters speculate on the writing of the script itself. Ronnie wonders why Steven wouldn't allow him to sing "In the Ghetto" twice: "That would have stretched things out" so that Steven wouldn't have to write as much, and "woulda added meaning" (whatever that means).[8] In the typewritten version of the script, and in the finished film, these characters are more "in character" and depressive, and do not interact with or seem aware of Steven. Like Steven's go-nowhere scripts, this impotent fantasy descends into violence.

Skip and Stanley play cards and drink as Ronnie stares out the window, while Dawn tries to get Skip to pay attention to her. Rebuffed, she dances by herself, then notices Ronnie watching her and signals him over in a bid to make Skip jealous. Skip glares at them as Ronnie lifts her skirt, and Stanley passes out, drunk. A disgusted Skip heads to the washroom, leaving Ronnie and Dawn alone with Stanley's limp body. Ronnie advances on Dawn, but she rebukes him. Skip then reveals that he is watching through the keyhole. He taunts and goads Dawn into letting Ronnie have his way with her, and she defiantly agrees. Ronnie, realizing that he's just a pawn in their game of sexual aggression, and furious over Skip's Elvis-themed jibes, drags Skip out of the washroom and into a fight. Stanley, knocked awake, reacts to the situation the only way he knows (smashing his head into the floor again and again) while Dawn takes Skip's side of the struggle. "Watch out! He's got karate!" she warns as Ronnie chops his way out of Skip's eye gouge. The comic violence escalates to brutality as Dawn rushes to Skip's defence by bludgeoning Ronnie to death with Steven's typewriter, thus ending his life with the device that gave him birth.

All of this takes place in Steven's imagining, not in his script, so there are no fresh yellow pages for him to discard. Instead, the typewriter makes its way into the trash can the next day. Just when all seems bleakest, Kim comes to the rescue. As the garbage truck hauls Steven's typewriter away, a copy of *Color Crime Quarterly* (also discarded) falls out onto the street. Kim picks it up and spies an advertisement by an "experienced script writer looking to collaborate with fresh talent." Kim responds to this ad by Dr C. Jolly by writing to the given address in the guise of Steven and including a picture. She fears that if something positive doesn't happen soon, the hillbillies in their trucks will come for Steven.

The good news that Dr Jolly wants to work with Steven – he mails back a bus ticket and motel reservation to meet him in Sails, Kansas, along with expense money – arrives on Steven's birthday. Both events necessitate another, more upbeat, party. The news is better than expected. The established script "doctor" wants to take Steven under his wing, and he already has great advice: "All the middles need are twists!" We'll soon uncover darkness beneath the doctor's advice, but for now, celebration is in order. In the original script version, the atmosphere is more foreboding. As Kim breaks the seemingly good news to Steven, lightning cracks and the wind howls.[9] Steven speaks as well, repeating "twists" in a mad howl.[10] Both elements (the storm and Steven's speech) are missing from the finished version of the film, in which Steven remains silent and the actual twists concerning Dr Jolly are more surprising because they are not foreboded.

Dr Jolly offers Steven the sort of inclusion he craves: the supposed chance to realize his amateur fantasies of "breaking in" to Hollywood (like many a would-be screenwriter, Steven believes that his spec screenplay will lead him to fame and fortune, no matter the cold realities of the marketplace then and now). Steven's dream of creating "Crime Wave" has brought about his exclusion from the wider social sphere, while his failure to create "Crime Wave" has granted him inclusion in the otherwise imaginary "Crime Wave Club." His real dream, though, is to "join the club" of Hollywood superstars who enjoy both commercial and artistic success. The irony of these dreams of inclusion and exclusion is that, by its nature as an independent Canadian feature, *Crime Wave* has already been excluded from the club. In the same way, the imaginary "Crime Wave," by virtue of being a "color crime movie," belongs to the club of paracinemas that exist (by definition) outside the cultural mainstream, where the success Steven wants might otherwise be found. "Crime Wave" can never realize Steven's dream, because its intended genre marks it as what Sconce calls "cinematic 'trash'"[11] in the same way that Paizs's copying of paracinematic surfaces marks *Crime Wave*.

When Kim reports the good news from Dr Jolly to Steven, he's staring at the walls, at one of his many posters for other "color crime" pictures, in this case *The Sellout* (1952). An odd comment on the American script doctor's advice: add twists, follow the Hollywood formulae, "sell out" your vision of crafting something unique that will tower above similar pictures. Don't try to make the *best* movie, just make *another* movie. Throughout the following "party" sequence, and in earlier scenes set in Steven's apartment, a host of such posters are visible. Although they rarely seem to serve as commentary in like manner, they do strengthen *Crime Wave*'s bond with "trash" cinema even as the establishment of this bond marks *Crime Wave* as a postmodern art film rather than a "color crime movie." The poster for *Teen-Age Crime Wave* (1955) appears to relate to the title of Paizs's film, but since there are no real teenagers in *Crime Wave*, it doesn't seem to have much larger relevance. Neither does *Hell's Island* (1955), although the latter was shot in "VistaVision," the sort of hyperbolic marketing term that Paizs is spoofing with terms like "Ultra-Focus." ("VistaVision" was a real format created by Paramount Pictures, which oriented the 35mm negative horizontally for finer-grained "vistas.")

It's worth noting that these posters are for real movies. A viewer might be forgiven for suspecting that *Canadian Mounties vs. Atomic Invaders* (1953) is a figment of Paizs's own imagination, but in fact it was a real serial produced by Republic Pictures. A Cold War drama, its "atomic invaders" were Soviets, not spacemen as the science fiction title seems to suggest. These posters point to the oddity of Paizs's avowed influences, which were posters and movie trailers for 1950s genre thrillers, rather than the actual movies (which Paizs found less exciting than their marketing materials). In a sense, Paizs's influences come from the paracinemas of paracinemas (posters, not movies – perhaps doubly "parasitic" in that sense, since Paizs's style draws its lifeblood from the discards of a discarded cinema culture). Paizs's copying in this scene takes a literal form – he has rephotographed these movie posters – that illustrates the generative potential of this style. The role that copying plays in theoretical discourse is worth recalling here. Just as Žižek finds it generative to "copy" Lacan, thus producing a Hegelian form of psychoanalytic discourse, Paizs copies American "junk" to postmodern-ize Canadian cinema. The notion is distinct from, and opposed to, the popular conception that copying produces a degenerative version, the way a photocopier degrades images. (A more literal exploration of this idea can be seen in the work of other Winnipeg Film Group artists from the same period. Ed Ackerman and Greg Zbitnew, in "a rebellion against the Film Group for procuring a copier for the office, as opposed to actual film equipment,"[12] produced *5¢ a Copy* [1980], an animated short film consisting of photocopied images.)

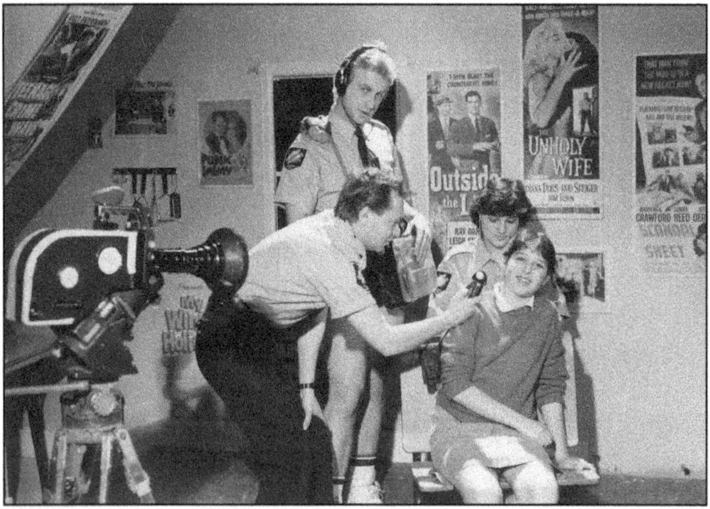

Gerry Klym, Jon Coutts, and Sylvia Kovacs help prepare Eva Kovacs – many "color crime" movie posters appear in the background. Courtesy of John Paizs, from the director's personal collection.

Paizs's distinctive aesthetic of "copying" extends, of course, beyond these posters and trailers into other realms. Paizs has stated that "when I first got my VCR, all I rented [was] bad science-fiction ... After I saw *Plan Nine From Outer Space* [1959], which opens with a narrator behind a desk, I reshot the scenes of Kim narrating, and put her behind a desk."[13] That Paizs's copying focuses on marginalized forms of "junk" culture links him to the "camp" aesthetic of figures like John Waters, an avowed influence, and further explains why he's often connected to Maddin. Yet just as Maddin does something more complicated, and less camp-y, through his rehabilitation of outmoded forms and genres, so does Paizs (whose films also lack an engagement in identity politics, a hallmark of camp). Paizs may be, as Mark Peranson suggests, "an assimilator of the detritus of popular culture,"[14] but his recombination of this material accords to a sober logic rather than a madcap silliness, due to the metafictional structure through which these recombinations cohere.

The Lacking Penny

A notable exception to the rule of movie posters that signal, within the film, to its real-world influences, is visible in the earlier sequence about the "Crime Wave" club. Cagle explains:

> While Paizs-as-Steven places himself among the characters he has created, he then goes one step further by including a poster of his own "The Three Worlds of Nick" trilogy placed inconspicuously among the other B-movie posters in his apartment. In fact, Paizs's name is only visible in one or two shots, and then, is nearly obscured by the bodies of the fighting men. Such a move ... serves to underscore the artificial nature of identity ... [and] points to the artificiality of Paizs's role-playing and creates ... a particular type of humour that arises from the incongruity between representation and reality.[15]

Here, through this intertextual reference, Paizs seems to be pointing also to the earlier "quiet man" films as part-and-parcel of *Crime Wave*'s world. The poster, which destabilizes Steven's diegetic identity through its presence by recalling his previous cinematic incarnations as Nick, seems at first to be in keeping with the postmodern conception of identity as artificial and in constant flux. But the presence of this poster, and the repetition of the "quiet man" figure, in fact suggests an identity that stands in a state of extreme fixity, or rather, an identity that depends on external regulation by some Other (in the metafictive reading of these films, this "Other" is none other than Paizs himself). Regarding the similarity of Steven and Nick, Paizs states:

> Nick and Steven are essentially the same character. And in *Springtime in Greenland* you see his alienation and read into it a longing to escape. But as yet there's no plan. In the next Nick film, *Oak, Ivy and other Dead Elms,* he's still the outsider. And you can see him trying to figure out who he is through his somewhat ill-considered hero-worship of his college roommate, the wasp-establishment, neoconservative and charismatic Brock West. The next Nick film, *The International Style,* is an escapist fantasy, and doesn't offer Nick/Steven any long enough term solution, and he winds up back where he started, in *Greenland*; but now with a wife and a baby on the way to support! But finally in *Crime Wave* he takes the bull by the horns – his style – and emerges victorious – again, his style.[16]

Although my reading of *Crime Wave* is at odds with Paizs's interpretation, since I argue in this book that Steven's "victory" is in fact ironic failure, I agree with this idea that Steven is essentially coextensive with Nick. Which raises the question: Is a character with a basic identity so stable that he can move from film to film, and name to name, virtually unchanged, in line with postmodern scepticism about stable identities?

What Paizs's 1980s "quiet man" films suggest, in fact, is a vision of identity more akin to the subject in Lacanian psychoanalysis (the subject as a lack, an empty space, a position defined by the dialectic between the empty subject and its external relations) than any subject in postmodern theory. The "quiet man" stands, rather, as a stable, fixed point in the psychic landscape of the film, somewhat inaccessible, created and re-created through a dialectical relationship to his situation/world. Žižek argues that

> in contrast to the notion that we are dealing with a subject the moment an entity displays signs of a phantasmatic "inner life" which cannot be reduced to external behaviour, one should claim that what characterizes subjectivity is rather *the gap which separates the two*: fantasy, at its most elementary, is inaccessible to the subject, and it is this inaccessibility which makes the subject "empty."[17]

The "quiet man" is far from any illustration or endorsement of psychoanalytic theory; the point here is that Paizs's work may make use of the techniques and tropes of postmodernism, but it does not cleanly align with the postmodernist world view. Billy/Nick/Steven seems to exist as a set of permutated qualities attached to a body (Paizs's own) and flattened to a filmed image, rather than the "normal" situation of a fictional character with illusory depth and emotional range. The "quiet man" thus appears "empty" in Žižek's sense – to "lack" character in the same way that, as Bruce Fink notes, "lack in Lacan's work has, to a certain extent, an ontological status: it is the first step beyond nothingness."[18] Unlike Billy and Nick, Steven seems on some level (as we see in his final beginning and ending) *aware* of his odd "existence." He later creates or copies himself inside his narrative (where he seems more self-aware than in the film's "reality"), in an anxious or perhaps paranoid imitation of his own creation by Paizs (who, we should remember, has imbued Penny with some of his own qualities).

The film does not dwell on such questions, but they become important to later interpretation of the final beginning and ending to "Crime Wave" that Steven will come to write. Beforehand, without any hints of this later anxiety, in a charming "party" sequence, Steven and Kim celebrate the news of Jolly's interest and Steven's birthday by two-stepping, drinking freezies, bopping balloons on their noses, and more good clean fun, which includes Steven swinging Kim around in an "airplane." Bucolic painted birds regard them from the window, announcing the turn away from reality with the possibility of writing "Crime Wave" and towards the unreal world of fantasy (which will later descend into nightmare). While Kim and Steven party, the soundtrack plays "Ice Box City," a peppy New Wave song by the then-popular Winnipeg band Popular Mechanix. The song directly references figures from pop culture (i.e., bodybuilder mogul Joe Weider) and media consumption (of "TV shows" and "porn flicks" – the version of the song in *Crime Wave* is truncated and doesn't get into the porn flicks, as if the soundtrack were aware of Kim listening). A lot of the charm of *Crime Wave*, especially in scenes like this one, lies in its home-made qualities of obvious artifice. However artificial its trappings, and however meticulous the process (anecdotal accounts of *Crime Wave*'s production always comment on Paizs's perfectionism), for Kim the production of *Crime Wave* must have been a lot of fun. As Paizs swings her through the air, she smiles in authentic glee.

5

Twists!

The party over, Kim drifts off to a peaceful sleep, as does Steven, with visions of "twists" drifting through his head (letters float through his window in an animated sequence, to form the word "twists" – Paizs produced this scene through a double exposure, first shooting the apartment set and then the animation stand).[1] In the original script, Steven lies awake as Ronnie Boyles, the Hollidays, and Stanley Falco carouse in the neighbourhood.[2] The original version of the film reduces this scene to the figures appearing in the darkness of the room. In both earlier versions (the scripted and the shot) these "Crime Wave" protagonists, excised from the finished film, whisper creepily that "tomorrow will be different."[3] Although Paizs has removed this creepy nod to coming threats, the finished film wastes no time offering us a disturbing "twist." The next day, Kim gives Steven a motherly send-off, combing his hair, handing him licorice, and demanding postcards from his travels. "Little did I know, that morning," she says, "that Dr C. Jolly, sometime after he placed that ad, would go crazy for no reason that anyone knew of."

This twist is so implausible and absurd that it can only be seen as Paizs himself taking Dr Jolly's advice. (Again, Paizs is ahead of his time: the same sudden, joking reliance on forced twists reappears in *Adaptation*, when the blocked writer Charlie Kaufman enlists his hack-writer brother Donald to complete his script. The plot of *Adaptation* then twists towards a Hollywood blockbuster ending for the until-then personal film that Charlie had been writing. *Adaptation* also features a scene where the struggling writer receives advice from a screenwriting guru, although Robert McKee is portrayed as much more stable than Dr Jolly. It would be interesting to know if Kaufman ever caught *Crime Wave* on late night television.) The implication of *Crime Wave*'s twists occurring in the wake of Jolly's advice to write twists into "Crime Wave" troubles the already shaky distinction between the two films. This unnatural turn of the plot and the film's concurrent shift in tone imply that *Crime Wave* is in fact "Crime Wave," a now-completed film, even though the final beginning and ending of Steven Penny's "Crime Wave" seem to insist on the impossibility of ever completing "Crime Wave" in any satisfactory manner. At the same time, as Steven travels deeper into the heart of Kansas and moves closer to crafting his final beginning and ending to "Crime Wave," *Crime Wave* becomes even less naturalistic. Exteriors and scenery, despite their "paracinematic" stylization, still have some (even if remote) connection to reality in the earlier moments of *Crime Wave*. However, as the film progresses, *Crime Wave* seems more and more to traffic in imagery with no meaningful connection to the world outside the film, as *Crime Wave* becomes increasingly self-referential. This aesthetic logic is already inherent in the repetition of paracinema surfaces, but as *Crime Wave* progresses, its "twists" transform paracinematic copying from an artistic technique into a narrative logic. *Crime Wave* spirals towards an unreality that culminates in its own disavowal.

Shifting Tones and Crossing Borders

Not long after this point in the film, *Crime Wave* lost its original audience. In part, this occurred because of the mechanical failure described earlier, but a contributing factor may have been the shift in tone that begins with the next scene. Until this point, *Crime Wave* has been a strange, unusual film, but aside from small moments of winking absurdity (e.g., the painted birds outside Steven's window in the party sequence), nothing in the story proper (i.e., Steven's narrative) has defied real-world possibility. After this point, events become somewhat fantastical (as when a street light, instead of crushing Steven's skull, magnifies his writing talent and transports him to Kim's bedroom), and the dark undertones rise to the surface. The original ending (examined in chapter 7) has a similar (even more extreme) shift in tone and is simply less funny than the new/current ending. As Jay Scott put it in the review that helped Paizs decide to reshoot this ending, "the tone [of the original] switches from mildly nuts and robustly funny to robustly nuts and mildly funny."[4] The current ending – the "official" ending described in this chapter and the next – switches the tone to robustly nuts and robustly funny, although it does preserve and extend many darker moments.

The first of these is the on-screen appearance of the crazed Dr Jolly. He speaks to his wife on a motel phone, while in the background, a man lays face-down on the bed, hogtied and blindfolded. Jolly's wife puts his son on the phone. The banality of the conversation makes this moment frightening, despite Jolly's comic-book craziness: "Hello, Sport. What's that? Not sweet enough? Well, that's why they call it unsweetened. You like oranges, don't you? Well, it's the same thing." This play-acting (with Jolly in the role of the family man on the road) is all the more perverse because of the relaxed, low-key conversation. In his book on David Lynch, Todd McGowan somewhat surprisingly aligns Lynch with the posture of normality, which is evident to him even in Lynch's mode of dress. McGowan sees Lynch as "taking normality to its logical extreme" to show "how the bizarre is not opposed to the normal but inherent within it."[5] McGowan argues that our "difficulty [with] Lynch's films does not lie so much in how subversive or radical they are, but in the fact that they offer a far more normal perspective than mainstream Hollywood film. They create an absolute division between social reality and fantasy, and this is a normality that we aren't used to seeing, either in Hollywood or in our everyday lives."[6] In offering a Dr Jolly who is both excessively normal (as shown by this conversation) and truly bizarre (as displayed by his perversity and violence), Paizs seems to be producing a Lynchian figure in McGowan's sense, and positing insanity and violence as the dark core of the American dream of Hollywood domination that Steven pursues. (We should remember, however, that Paizs's work precedes most of Lynch's own developments along these lines.) However, Paizs does not hold the worlds of social reality and fantasy apart from each other in the Lynchian method; rather, he subjects them to a postmodern collapse.

After concluding his conversation, Dr Jolly approaches the bed. Humming Gene Autry's "Back in the Saddle Again" (the tune that Skip whistled earlier, as he bound Dawn), Jolly "saddles up" atop the prone man. He has affixed the photo of Steven Penny that Kim sent him to the back of the man's head, and stares at this while he shakes the man awake. The wakened man tries to shake him off, but Jolly bucks against the man's back, crazily singing his country song. Jolly has donned a white cowboy hat, and since the two characters are played by the same actor, this recalls the tribute artist "Hank" from Steven's first beginning to "Crime Wave," as noted above – he's even singing a country song. Steven's violent imaginings have now come to horrifying life.

It is significant that this occurs as he crosses the border, entering America. In many respects, Steven's journey to America is an inversion of Dorothy's journey to Oz. As Pevere writes:

> Steven's eerie trip to the post-apocalyptic, chemically-poisoned night-world of *Crime Wave*'s Kansas is a logical and profoundly resonant extension of the hitherto purely comic descent into the media melting-pot.

> The trip to America is, for Steven and the countless couch-potato Canadians he represents, a kind of journey to a subconscious homeland, which, like Oz's Emerald City, represents something as mysterious and alien as it is magical and magnetic. Simultaneously Steven is confronted both with his desire for and his difference from the media-created world of America he's so desperately wanted to be part of (a condition of cultural schizophrenia as characteristically Canadian as any other factor of our much-stalked identity).[7]

Steven's journey to Kansas is both parallel to and distinct from Dorothy's journey to Oz. Steven heads to Kansas (whereas Dorothy leaves it), seeking his "wizard" script doctor. Steven searches not for a way home but for a way to flee forever. Like Scarecrow, Lion, and Tin Man, Steven believes the doctor will make him whole, fill in the lack he feels (giving him not a brain, courage, or a heart, but middles). And like Dorothy, he will discover that the man behind the curtain is a fraud.

In their ultimate confrontation, Dr Jolly taunts Steven with Jolly's own inability to measure up to Steven's fantasy: "Am I what you expected?" As it happens, unlike the Wizard, Dr Jolly is *more* than Steven expects, not less: he is something more powerful, more threatening, a serial killer more disturbed and more gleeful than the ones he has imagined in his scripts, and just as merciless. An author of violence in his own right, Dr Jolly is more "established" (as his advertisement proclaimed), his violence real. He possesses his own dream. In their coming confrontation, Dr Jolly reveals that dream to Steven: "I've never wanted anything so badly as to show you what I mean by 'twists.'"

Not in Canada Anymore

The trip to see Dr Jolly, like Dorothy's trip to see the Wizard, is fraught, although it begins sunnily enough. Steven sends Kim the postcards she has demanded, and the friendly bus driver allows Steven to take the wheel for a while, even though he almost drives into oncoming traffic. The bus sequence combines a stolen shot of an actual Grey Goose bus with "an 'in-studio' shot, a steering wheel from an auto wreckers in [Paizs's] hands, and shaky camera to complete the effect."[8] Triumphant music blares on the soundtrack during this sequence – although the film seems to anticipate victory, the viewer can recognize this tune as a sunnier version of Dr Jolly's mad Autry singsong, so it strikes another ironic chord. Then, in a further twist, a state trooper stops Steven's bus just ten miles from his destination. (Here, Paizs pulls off another trick: "We see, ostensibly, the shadow of the bus appear on the road as the bus comes to a stop there just out of frame. In reality, however, the shadow was created by holding a broad sheet of Styrofoam up high in the middle of the road and walking it into position. That combined with the bus sound effect sold the illusion."[9]) When Penny disembarks from the bus, Paizs is really just stepping off an apple crate and pretending to hold an imaginary handrail.[10]

Nobody is allowed into Sails, where Steven has arranged to meet the doctor. The police won't say why, but Kim fills us in: "What was happening in Sails was that something escaped into the air from a closeby secret place and everyone had to leave their homes fast. Secret stuff fell all over everything and if someone's dog or cat was left behind it was too bad for their dog or cat." Like her explanation for Dr Jolly's sudden insanity ("for no reason that anyone knew"), the language here is excessively vague – the kind you would put into the first draft of your screenplay and later replace. But it hasn't been replaced. On one level, this vagueness is appropriate to Kim's childlike inability to really understand what's happening. On another level, in a metafictional film about screenwriting failures, such vagueness seems humorous and thematically appropriate. On yet another level, *Crime Wave* has managed to absorb more elements into its pastiche through the addition of not just the cliché of the deranged serial killer but this science fiction B-movie plot device. (Earlier, with *Ed Zorax of the Future City*, and later, with *Top of the Food Chain*, Paizs took the "tribute artist" approach to science fiction films more completely.)

While Kim reports this new development, we're treated to the townscape of Sails, another image that is painted on glass (like the birds sunning themselves outside of Steven's window during the birthday party scene). This same background image appeared in the film earlier, on the brochure for the "Sails Motor Cove" sent to Steven by Jolly. As Steven draws closer to his fantasy (until enveloped by it, drawn into his script as its protagonist), the world around him seems to redraw itself in line with the media he has consumed. The scene's backdrop copies the cultural "trash" of a travel brochure in the same way that Paizs copies paracinematic "trash." Paizs's repetition of imagery within the film also emphasizes the growing power of Steven's fantasy, which approaches critical mass and collapse while undermining the possibility of separation between narrative levels. The township of Sails – a mass of billboards and corporate logos, a toxic land so synthetic it has noticeably been hand-drawn – is also the film's only distinctively American landscape. Aggressively artificial and overly corporate, this dreamscape seems pulled from the Canadian imagination and seems impossible to read except as satirical critique. But what is being critiqued? Canadian stereotypes of America as much as any American cultural reality. In the middle of this landscape, which is doubly toxic since it's overwhelmed by both corporate imagery and "secret stuff," government agents in yellow jumpsuits and gas masks shoot wayward dogs.

We could connect these figures, through the colour yellow, to the yellow pages of Penny's script, but symbolically this doesn't accomplish much (and we would then, as well, need to connect Kim's own yellow raincoat). We might note, however, that these bright yellows contribute to the high-contrast tones of the film's faux-Technicolor aesthetic, which remains one of Paizs's enduring stylistic innovations. Director Solomon Nagler, one of the brightest stars of the Winnipeg Film Group's later era, rejects the aesthetic of earlier Winnipeg Film Group figures like Paizs, yet he acknowledges Paizs's influence: "The use of high contrast mise-en-scène was first introduced [to the films of the Winnipeg Film Group] in the post-modern suburban angst films of John Paizs and was later picked up by the Cronus of the Winnipeg film scene, Guy Maddin, who extended it onto a self-referential manipulation of the celluloid material."[11] Throughout the 1990s and 2000s, the Winnipeg Film Group's best directors were still recognizing and responding to the work Paizs had produced in the 1980s.

Fateful Meetings

The police also stop Dr Jolly because of the events in Sails, and Jolly finds himself trapped between a policeman and one of those ever-troublesome truck-driving hillbillies. This hillbilly wants to breed his dog, the daintily named Polo, who sits in the passenger seat while his wife lies in the truck's box. After the dog begins barking at Dr Jolly's trunk (where the body of his last victim is bundled into a garbage bag), the doctor speeds away. Jolly almost runs down the policeman, which initiates a car chase (again, bringing to life a recurring element from Steven's failed scripts, the cliché of the "chase scene"). Jolly soon loses the officer by driving into a sunflower field. He abandons the car and, also like Steven, continues on foot along a barbed wire fence, careful not to step over into the contaminated area surrounding Sails.

The fence that Steven and Jolly follow, each heading towards the other, is a temporary, government fence, a series of white wooden X's with barbed wire strung between them. As Steven marches along the fence, and the day fades into night, the cheerful marching music ("For He's a Jolly Good Fellow") that accompanies his steps becomes more

"Hillbillies" (Cookie) Roscoe Handford and Greg Klymkiw (producer of many early films by John Paizs and Guy Maddin and subject of the 2013 documentary *Survival Lessons: The Greg Klymkiw Story*). Courtesy of John Paizs, from the director's personal collection.

Dr Jolly (Neil Lawrie) being filmed by Tom Fijal, with Gerry Klym behind some sunflowers. Courtesy of John Paizs, from the director's personal collection.

discordant. It sounds as if a marching band has followed Steven but, growing tired, has fallen out of step and out of tune until giving up altogether as Steven himself stumbles and falls. Half-raising himself off the ground, Steven gasps in a tableau shot with a white X fencepost just behind and to the left of him, body slanted like the X. This *mise en scène* makes the temporary fencepost seem like a cross that Steven has carried, the burden of which has caused him to collapse in imitation of Jesus. There is a progression of iconography here – first Ronnie Boyles, a Penny stand-in, is "crucified" face-first on a telephone pole, and now Steven has collapsed beneath this "cross" while struggling onward towards the place where Jolly plans to kill him. Later, in Steven's imagined final ending to "Crime Wave," Jesus will appear in his darkest hour; Steven will then imitate Jesus by forgiving Dr Jolly and washing his feet. It's hard to take any of this seriously. Steven does not suffer for his art – instead, he gives up on it, and only soldiers forth in this moment because he has bought into America's quick-fix mentality, outsourcing his artistry and inspiration to the script doctor. If anything, and especially if Kim and Steven have co-produced *Crime Wave* to tell the story of how Steven came to write "Crime Wave," such moments suggest how Steven views himself and ask us to laugh at, rather than pity, Steven in his pain.

As night falls, Steven stumbles across another street light, one already lit with brilliance. He basks in this light, certain of inspiration, filled with hope, but impatient. He pulls on a sweater against the cold, settles in with some licorice for the night – and then feels or hears something, a figure in the darkness, walking towards him along the fence. He waves, and Dr Jolly waves back. Steven, excited, rehearses his handshake and fidgets with nervous excitement. His smile fades as Dr Jolly steps into the light and Steven sees, in an instant, that the doctor is insane.

The next scene of *Crime Wave* has odd similarities to the "cowboy" scene in David Lynch's *Mulholland Dr.* (2001), and tempts one to wonder if Lynch had seen Paizs's film. In *Mulholland Dr.*, a film director who is (also) attempting to make a 1950s-esque feature film ends up meeting with a strange figure known as "the cowboy" (like Dr Jolly, a pale, thin man in a comically large, white cowboy hat) to discuss the making of this film. Their meeting (also) takes place at night, underneath an overhead light, one that flickers and buzzes to life (like the earlier street lights in *Crime Wave*). Similarly, both scenes by Lynch and Paizs oscillate in tone between comic absurdity and sinister threat. The sudden tonal shifts throughout *Crime Wave* rival Lynch's own, although Lynch in his films often sacrifices sense for tone, whereas Paizs's narrative structures possess a surface clarity that belies their metafictive tangles. Although *Crime Wave* may seem at times like "*Blue Velvet* for kids,"[12] and Paizs himself has noted similarities between the two films, *Blue Velvet* (1986) appeared in the time between *Crime Wave*'s premiere and its re-release with a new ending. Again, Paizs and *Crime Wave* fell victim to bad timing, as Paizs notes:

> *Crime Wave* is set in this *Leave It to Beaver* world, which was the shocking idea in *Blue Velvet*, and one I had already used in *Springtime in Greenland*. But because I was unknown, *Crime Wave* is not part of the mythology. *Blue Velvet* upset me. I was almost finished *Crime Wave* and I'm sitting in the audience watching Lynch's film. Suddenly, there's that white picket fence and the same kind of imagery I was working with. I could not fucking believe it![13]

Paizs's exasperation is echoed by Mark Peranson, who speculates that "*Blue Velvet*'s success, along with Tim Burton's absurdist *Pee Wee's Big Adventure* [1985], may even have something to do with the failure of *Crime Wave* as some critics unfairly wrote Paizs off as an imitator."[14] The ending of Burton's film finds Pee Wee at the drive-in, watching a movie based on his own story (the preceding events of the film), a twist of a different order but with some outward similarities to Steven Penny's insertion of himself into the final beginning and ending of "Crime Wave." Burton's own metafictional flourishes and moments of bright, stylized pastiche, and Lynch's examination of the violence and darkness beneath such surfaces, find earlier expression in these 1980s films by Paizs.

As already noted, Dr Jolly begins their meeting by taunting Steven. Jolly finds Steven less than he expected: the doctor believed he would be "bigger," with "broader shoulders." "Hard to tell from a picture," says Jolly, and herein lies the crux of *Crime Wave*, the idea on which it rotates – a gap persists between Steven's reality and his fantasy, but also between what the camera presents as the diegetic reality and what the film suggests of its narrative structure, and these gaps cause fundamental instabilities. We see only pictures – 24 each second – and can't possibly know what stirs in the darkness between them, beyond the street light, beneath Steven's silence. What meaning can we glean from the fact that we view blackness longer than we view the filmed world? The gulf between Steven's dreams (of worldwide color crime movie domination) and his reality (as a non-professional filmmaker stuck in Winnipeg, without the talent or resources to break out) stands so wide that it cannot be closed, and through that gap issues a film that ironically takes its own impossibility as its subject and foundation. Steven's dreams are so big that even in the fantasies of his final beginning and ending he will fail to be satisfied with their realization. "Am I what you expected?" Jolly asks, and of course he is not, but this obscures how Jolly brings Steven's violent fantasies to life. Jolly reveals his own perverse dream – to show Steven what he means by "twists" – as he draws out and breaks apart the word "twisssssss ssttss," snakelike, in the same way that Steven will later break apart the word "real ly" on his typewriter, an aural gap to match the later written one.

New Hope through Electrocution

Jolly lunges for Steven's throat, and Paizs cuts to Kim startled awake – as if, Dorothy-like, she has dreamed this alien Kansas. The film does become more dreamlike at this point, as its script undergoes another twist. Has Kim authored these twists, taken control of Steven's script in her attempt to save him? Since Kim later reveals that she has learned to write middles, we cannot discount this possibility, although it would further destabilize the film's narrative levels, rather than aligning them. In any case, Kim reveals the next twist, a *deus ex machina* ending, through her narration: "That night I knew that Steven was in very great danger. What I didn't know was that thanks to a series of strange and fantastic happenings, Steven would be transformed!"

The film cuts back to Jolly's lunge at Steven, interrupted by Polo the dog, now magically evolved through contact with the "secret stuff." Polo drives the truck towards the two (the dog-breeding hillbillies trail on foot) and crashes into the street light. The collision knocks out Dr Jolly, who will confess to his crimes when discovered and captured by the police. However, Kim announces, "[the police] wouldn't find [Steven] because there was no more Steven. At least not the Steven we last knew, my friend who couldn't write middles and who saw his every last hope go bad. No, they wouldn't find that Steven, because thanks to a Kansas street light he was given the strength of the world and the power of a wonderful new beginning!"

While Kim's enervating narration unfurls, we see Steven being electrocuted, the street light having landed to crush his skull in another fateful meeting. But instead of killing Steven, this street light somehow fuses with his being to grant him the aforementioned powers. Paizs has noted that his films and their "compositions and attention to detail were definitely informed by my comic book roots, as was … the sequential storytelling through still images technique that they combined to

"Polo" (Tara) garners attention on set. Courtesy of John Paizs, from the director's personal collection.

create. That's right out of a comic book."[15] This bizarre twist follows the narrative logic of a superhero origin story: the hero suffers a freak accident that should kill him but instead grants him superpowers.

Unlike the street light seen earlier, which was fabricated by Paizs, "the street light on Steven's head was an actual (disused) street light" that Paizs received from the City of Winnipeg.[16] Paizs notes that he "had an artist friend who makes glass sculptures cut the hole in the lens. Then I screwed a hockey helmet into the shell. My head went into the hockey helmet. A small lightbulb wrapped in red cellophane, and connected to a dimmer, provided the glow."[17] The resulting image recalls a superhero's costume helmet, just as the event recalls an origin story. Note that it is here, when we might expect a fake street light, that Paizs uses a real one, whereas earlier, when the street light seems real, it is fake. Such occurrences flow from the exigencies and demands of the production process; that said, the result is a film whose thematic concerns with copying and unreality find unusual echoes in its production processes.

A more striking confluence between the production process and the filmed images it produces appears after, street light on skull, Steven transports himself somehow to Kim's bedroom. After calming the frightened Kim, Steven wills the darkened, broken street light crowning him to brilliance, and settles over her typewriter to write the final beginning and ending to "Crime Wave." This typewriter, before becoming a prop in *Crime Wave*, had been used by Paizs to write *Crime Wave*.[18] That Steven now settles over the same typewriter that gave him life, in order to write his own "Crime Wave" (in which he "gives himself life" in a similar fashion), is noteworthy not just for this real-world parallel between Paizs and Penny, but also because of the metafictional dimension of the final beginning and ending that Steven Penny will produce.

Since Steven writes himself into "Crime Wave" at this point, on the same typewriter that Paizs used to write Steven into *Crime Wave*, we can read this final revision of "Crime Wave" as Steven's own revision of *Crime Wave* and therefore of his own self. Simply put, Steven Penny is re-writing John Paizs's script and attempting to revise his own identity in the process. The circumstances of the film's production – the fact that Paizs replaced the original ending with the new ending that the film is about to reveal – would lend a strange air of prophecy to the scene, if not for the fact that this revision of the ending to "Crime Wave" is in fact the *revised* ending to *Crime Wave*.

In the metafictional reading, then, where Steven has finally taken over the script to the very film in which he stars, in supposed triumph, he does so unaware that he has already failed – or rather, that in the original film's ending, he succeeded, and Paizs *cut his success out of the finished film*. Steven's final scripted ending, in which he draws close enough to his fantasy to uncover the horror of its impossibility, resonates more fully for an audience sensitive to the production's history. Beyond Steven's sad admission of failure, the "lost" reel of his triumph hovers, spectral.

6

The Gap Exposing the Real

The final beginning and ending of "Crime Wave" breaks from the formula of its precursors in important ways. Most obviously, it presents a self-reflexive metafiction (not unlike Paizs's own *Crime Wave*) in place of the typical crime plot. Steven Penny imagines himself as the protagonist of the film-within-a-film, and the "Crime Wave" within *Crime Wave* becomes the story of "Steven Penny" and his rise to color crime moviemaking supremacy. An unlikely hero hailing "from the North" (this phrase, reiterated from Steven's previous beginnings, is grafted onto the cover of *Time* magazine), "Steven Penny" rockets south (from Canada) into Hollywood and international superstardom. Instead of using a metaphorical stand-in, Steven plunks himself into the script (although, in turn, we might read Steven as a metaphorical stand-in for Paizs). "Steven" as a protagonist has no peers, no competitors in the color crime moviemaking racket. As the narrator notes, "only one guy truly made it" to the Top: "Steven Penny."

By inserting himself into this final beginning and ending, Steven gives birth to his own doppelgänger, producing a fantasy figure of himself that can enjoy the success he fails to achieve – yet even in this dreamed version, "Steven" cannot in fact "enjoy" anything. Freud argues that "the 'double' was originally an insurance against the destruction of the ego ... [but] reverses its aspect. From having been an assurance of immortality, it becomes the uncanny harbinger of death."[1] The appearance of Steven's double in his final scripted scenes for "Crime Wave" operates as just such a "harbinger": given the formula already established by Steven's previous drafts, the "beginning" will concern the childhood development of "Steven" into a filmmaker (his "first fateful steps"), and its "ending" will involve his death. Just as the appearance of Steven's double within his script implies his death from the moment of its entrance, Steven's placement of himself inside the script for "Crime Wave" signals a further "giving up" on color crime movies and thus the death of his dream, the failure of his fantasy. In *Crime Wave*'s ultimate ironic move, only through the creation of the script he's thus far laboured to produce does Steven Penny confirm and ensconce his failure to produce this script, through sarcastic testaments to his triumph.

The First Fateful Steps

"Steven" begins his rise to the top in the womb. As his pregnant mother attends an "all color crime movie bill," this quiet man speaks his only sentence of the film, as a fetus: "I can do better!" The narrator informs us that "the time for talk had passed – now was time for action!" Thus the film finally offers an explanation for Steven's silence, his "quiet man" status, albeit a ridiculous one, with "Steven" still unborn. The appearance of this "explanation" for Steven's senseless silence confirms the phantasmatic nature of this final beginning and ending. Fantasy ensconces disturbing elements into a narrative where, given places and functions, they cease to be traumatic. Steven's silence (which otherwise disturbs the film's surface, marking it as distinct from both the mainstream cinema "racket" that "Crime Wave" seeks to dominate and the paracinemas that *Crime Wave* strives to copy) is similarly absorbed into and given a place within the narrative of this "final" script.

Likewise, the narrator trumpets that "once on the outside, little Steven's zest for life could hardly be contained." The visual proof of this "zest for life" consists of "Steven" sitting, a silent baby, almost motionless. As in the other beginnings and endings, the film maintains an ironic distance between the narrator's speech or attitude and the images we see, but in this final beginning and ending the distance has grown – more importantly, in the ending it becomes clear that Steven now shares our viewpoint and regards himself from a detached, ironic distance. We're told that "as Steven grew, so did his imagination," but this increased imagination is established as negative. In a chilling scene that Paizs drops masterfully into the midst of the comedy, with a deftness to rival the sudden shifts of mood that have become Lynch's stock-in-trade, the young "Steven" switches off the television set – only to be draped in silence and darkness. The television within the shot had served as the source of the diegetic lighting in the scene (aside from the evening light filtered through the window), and as the source of the hitherto non-diegetic sound that had continued from previous scenes into this one. As in the earlier scene where the mailman whistles the tune that has just served as the score, Paizs here troubles the boundary that separates the diegetic world from its fictional frame. Not only in its metafictional structure (here, a film-within-a-film), but also in its form, style, and score, *Crime Wave* collapses distinctions between its inside and its outside.

Suddenly, we sit in silence and darkness, without the bombastic narrator, over-the-top music, or saturated "TotalColor." The film has ruptured, as if we are no longer watching a documentary clip from the beginning of "Crime Wave" but are witnessing the immediate experience of "Steven" as a child. For the first time, we get a glimpse of his inner world – his fear and his solitude – as he stands in the living room, alone, without anything to protect or distract him from his darker imaginings. The echoing roar of an unseen monster erupts, and "Steven" switches the television back on, returning to idyllic fantasies of worldwide color crime movie domination. A variation on this scene repeats soon after. This time "Steven" has donned a Superman outfit. (His dressing up as an American hero recalls the previous "street light costume" and foreshadows his later "dressing up" as a Steven Spielberg clone, complete with baseball cap.) He crawls into bed before switching the light out, and finds himself greeted once more by darkness and monstrous howling. He switches the light on more quickly this time. What should we make of his growing imagination, his final surrender to fantasy? Whenever the lights go out it becomes dark and quiet, as if in a movie theatre before the film begins. His imagination terrifies him, brings forth monsters.

The first steps "Steven" takes towards achieving worldwide color crime movie domination are likewise unexpected: with his first movie camera, "Steven" crafts a grainy, almost colourless, examination of the toilet bowl and its contents. He presents the film to his alarmed parents while rocking and clasping his hands together, looking at once like a child playing artist and a child traumatized. This first audience of alarmed parents (present in Steven's fantasies, but absent in the rest of the film) sit unimpressed. Perhaps they aren't Freudians – we seem cued in these scenes to read Steven's perfectionist difficulties as a species of anal retentiveness, and his desire for domination as an overcompensation for his self-perceived failures and fears. In the scripted version of this scene, he "rocks back and forth, slapping the backs of his ears,"[2] in a suggestion of autistic focus. His film does not consist of feces but of "seemingly ordinary phenomenon"[3] that, as the narrator also tells us in the scripted scene, fascinate "Steven" but pass unnoticed by others. This "origin story" conforms to the standard stereotype of the "sensitive artist," the cultural fantasy of artistic perception that serves to glorify artistic figures while excluding them from the "normal" social order, justifying their marginalization and poverty while excusing society from the burden of having to "see" value or meaning in the

Randolph Peters (original music) and Clive Perry (re-recording). The sound in *Crime Wave* both contributes to Paizs's pastiche and complicates the narrative structure. Courtesy of John Paizs, from the director's personal collection.

art they produce. The examples of such "seemingly ordinary phenomenon" that "Steven" parades as his "first world premiere" sound like the so-called marvels of "The House of Tomorrow": "stairs; car exhaust; water draining."[4] Thus his first film, in an unshot scene from the script, mimics the distinctive style of Paizs's previous 1980s films, which often feature still shots of objects in a series.

How does "Steven" get from these early moments to the heights of world domination? We can't know, unless we consider *Crime Wave* itself as filling the gap, as the "middle" link in this chain. Kim later encourages this interpretation, which makes it seem reasonable, but his story does not end with world domination. Like all of the previous endings of "Crime Wave," it ends with the protagonist's death.

The Final Words of Citizen Penny

The final ending of "Crime Wave" begins as a parody of *Citizen Kane* (1941). Like Welles's film, this ending opens with the sad, isolated death of a man ("Steven") who has soared to the absolute heights. Greg Klymkiw compares the two films: "I like to think of *Crime Wave* as the *Citizen Kane* of Canadian film history."[5] Like Kane, "Steven" leaves behind mysterious last words: since he's a quiet man, instead of whispering them, he types them out: "I real ly did mean to be good." This gap in "really" separates out the word "real" and suggests that space as the one from which the film issues. Even as the narrator returns to laud his life, offering an idealized portrait of the man that seems ludicrous in its epic proportions, the dream that is Steven Penny's final beginning and ending to "Crime Wave" seems to realize its own impossibility and inscribes within its fantasy space the "real" of its falsity. As the "final" ending of "Crime Wave" progresses, this fantasy expands and contracts, gasping for imaginative life. Each wish fulfilled brings Steven nothing but the most temporary pleasure – nothing "real" – although he seems to authentically desire these things in the moment, "mean[ing] to be good" in each case. Immediately after the narrator reports each achievement, he reports its failure to satisfy "Steven." The dream of Steven's ending begins to one-up itself, striving and then failing to outdo its previous extravagant success.

Kane-like, the narrator returns in a newsreel, now puzzled. "Steven" has realized all of his dreams: he has "had nothing but success" and has even graced the cover of his favourite magazine, *Color Crime Quarterly*. His success begins with a "trio of blockbuster features" that rehabilitate the discarded versions of "Crime Wave": *Special Agent* offers the story of Ronnie Boyles, *Just Like Us* tells the tale of the Hollidays, and even poor Stanley Falco returns a changed man, decisive and ready to take action as the Rambo-esque star of *The Last White Man in South Africa*. The scene with the Hollidays from *Just Like Us* begins comically, with Dawn unwrapping a birthday cucumber to light-hearted joking from a friendly couple. The tone shifts into heartfelt schmaltz, as Skip offers his present. Next, the tone darkens: Skip has gifted Dawn with photographs of her having sex with the unnamed male friend in the room. Skip laughs maniacally as he takes photographs of Dawn looking at these photographs of her (in one of them, the man is taking his own lewd photographs of Dawn).

In this moment, and throughout its incessant metafictional obsession with visual media, *Crime Wave* emphasizes how these media mediate desires and become objects of desire themselves. Visual media thus obstruct, even as they establish, social and sexual relationships. Jameson has noted that "whenever other media appear within film, their deeper function is to set off and demonstrate the latter's ontological primacy."[6] However, photographs within a film within a film within a film, offered by one character as proof of what happened "in reality," do not so much demonstrate the primacy of any medium as posit "reality" as always mediated (through technology, fantasy, neurobiology, etc.) and therefore inaccessible – which underlines the absurdity of attempts to locate "truth" in and through media. This includes, of course, the operation of looking to Steven's final beginning and ending of "Crime Wave" for indications of his actual victory over the script.

We might suspect, even if the narrator does not, that the remorse "Steven" expresses in these final words has to do with the subject matter of his movies. Sensationalist, even racist (Stanley Falco, the last white man in South Africa, snipers off-screen "bastards"), these now-completed crime movies are even more violent than their failed scripts suggested they might be. Clips play out on a screen before a bloodthirsty audience raving for more. Paizs produced this shot through another "double exposure. The actual movie screen as filmed was maybe a foot across. The patron holding up the baby is Randolph Peters, the composer of *Crime Wave*'s score."[7] In one of Penny's movies, as seen in this montage, the flesh of a woman's back is ripped away by hand. Although he disturbs in this moment, Paizs remains too conscious of his genre to stray from comedy for long, and follows with a cartoonish exploding head, in tribute to Cronenberg's *Scanners* (1981). The allusion to Cronenberg is intentional,[8] and appropriate. Cronenberg holds outsider status in Canadian film history as a result of having accomplished the dream that Steven Penny seeks: taking an American approach to a film genre (in Cronenberg's case, horror) but developing a distinctive, personal style, and triumphing both commercially and critically through genre mastery. But Penny is no Cronenberg. One of the narrator's lines, cut from the film but present in the script, explains that "Steven" produced "brand new titles, sequels, sequels to sequels, re-makes and special editions."[9] Although this line was cut from the film, it's still clear that these movies rely on clichés and recycled ideas. However, his lack of artistry suggests something other than the postmodern pastiche of Paizs's own copying, something more akin to Hollywood banality, the "degenerative" copying of xerographic technology.

One of the reasons for the disparity between the narrator's point of view and the perspective the images suggest has to do with the fact that our narrator views success as primarily commercial: "Whatever one uses to measure success – the dollar, pound, deutschmark or yen – the sum total of Steven Penny's career to that point came to one thing: he did good!" When the narrator stops to consider any non-material markers of success, he can only present clichés that commercialize these concepts as well. Success is a quality gained through the "possession" of respect or love: industry awards (which inevitably "came to mean less and less to Steven"); simply being cool (we see "Steven" playing blues harmonica in a nightclub); a lovely young wife (insert photo of an overdeveloped bodybuilder with big hair in a tiny bikini); a beautiful old home (the narrator seems to regard this material possession as somehow outside the commercial realm); and children ("two little angels on earth"). All along, this "everyman" director doesn't lose touch with his roots (here "Steven" wanders casually around a film set complete with Spielberg beard and cap). "Steven" seems to have other criteria for success, locked away behind his impassive face. As soon as he realizes a dream, in this final ending, "Steven" becomes bored and must move on. The narrator then offers the ultimate achievement, to trump all else: a theme park.

Insipid, pathetic, and distinctly American (the balloons floating above Steven Penny World are red, white, and blue), this dream of a theme park gets summed up in the next visual: an overweight impersonator of Ronnie Boyles, the Elvis impersonator, greets tourists at its gates. A copy of a copy of a copy, completely removed from anything possibly authentic that "Steven" might truly desire (while Paizs might unabashedly "copy," albeit in a way he views as original, Steven appears conflicted over his own, unoriginal, copying). We can thus detect, in *Crime Wave*, an anxiety that separates the film from any number of less successful postmodern dramas: for all of its surface value and aggressive artificiality, for all of its winking nods to its own unreality and to junk culture, within the black screen that underlies *Crime Wave*'s TotalColor surface swarms self-doubt about the possible emptiness and potential meaninglessness of postmodern posturing. Another scene cut in the transition from script to screen condenses this dark vision. Steven Penny World offers visitors "a thought provoking look into the future ... a smoking pit."[10]

"Steven" spends his time between establishing his theme park and his demise waiting for death. The penthouse apartment where "Steven" shuffles and sighs was, Paizs reports, "the 'royal suite,' where the Queen would stay in Winnipeg, at the Westin hotel ... at Portage and Main. The hotel let me use it for free. (It's amazing how many folks chipped in stuff for free in these pre-'Hollywood North' days. Doubt it would happen today.)"[11] Paizs's mocking use of the term "Hollywood North" – oft-repeated in Winnipeg by well-meaning sloganeers to refer to the city's service-industry film trade – suggests a further irony. Without pioneers like Paizs and Maddin, who put Winnipeg on the filmmaking map by forging decidedly non-Hollywood efforts, the city might never have developed this Hollywood service industry – which makes scheduling and financing the independent shoots that are the legacy of Paizs and Maddin more difficult than ever, since talent gets gobbled up by visiting productions and "freebies" are harder to come by. The exterior shot of the penthouse required less reliance on corporate charity: Paizs simply shot "a photograph of the Sherry-Netherland hotel in NY, NY, which I had found in a book at the library" that is now Winnipeg's Millennium Library.[12]

In this Royal penthouse, fit for a queen, an aging "Steven" – "aimless, tired, napping often" – looks listlessly through his wardrobe. The wardrobe is filled with Paizs's costume changes from the film's earlier scenes – the narrator remarks that "Steven" sees in this wardrobe "his life passing before him like a parade." The costumes Paizs has put on throughout the film come to symbolize the identities that "Steven" has put on throughout his imagined life; donning them equates with the postmodern conception of identity as a series of masks to be donned, none of which are accorded any "real" status, and which hide not the subject's true identity but the absence of anything "behind the mask." As noted earlier, Lacanian thought grants this "lack" an ontological status: "the very process of shifting among multiple identifications presupposes a kind of empty band which makes the leap from one identity to another possible, and this empty band is the subject itself."[13] Thus the "quiet man" moves from film to film, costume to costume, role to role.

"Steven" sits at his typewriter once again, still stricken with writer's block, even in his fantasy, as he begins his traumatic approach to its core. "Steven" cannot imagine anything further; he is now trapped within this ideal but somehow unsatisfactory ending. But what could he be trying to write? The answer is never given, but nevertheless plain: "Crime Wave," the film he has still not made in all of this fantasizing, the film that will tower above all others and earn the "real" success he so desires yet cannot enjoy even in his fantasies. Steven wants to realize "Crime Wave" in reality – but what does this mean in postmodernity? Where can one locate reality in a film with a metafictional structure as convoluted as *Crime Wave*'s? "I real ly did mean to be good." This admission puzzles the narrator, but on at least one level, it produces dramatic irony. The audience might grasp the meaning of these words, although the narrator cannot. "Steven" meant to craft the masterpiece "Crime Wave," not those banal blockbusters.

"Did the bitch-goddess Success claim another victim?" asks the narrator, in his best attempt to grasp how "Steven" has failed to overcome this impossible deadlock. The simple final words of "Steven Penny" counteract the extremity of his fantasy, dispelling it in a small, poignant apology for his giant, exemplary life. This seems inevitable from the moment that Steven writes himself into his script. In Žižek's terms, Steven castrates himself through the figure of his double: "Let us imagine a situation in which the subject aims at X (say, a series of pleasurable experiences); the operation of castration does not consist in depriving him of any of these experiences, but adds to the series a purely potential, nonexistent X, with respect to which the actually accessible experiences appear all of a sudden as lacking, not wholly satisfying."[14] This description encapsulates the narrative structure of Steven's final ending, which balloons success upon success until the entire fantasy bursts. The "X" of the series is the impossible accomplishment on which this fantasy depends. To sustain itself, Steven's fantasy of success must repress its impossibility by shunting it into a nonexistent "middle." What happens in this middle? What shot "Steven" from childhood precociousness to worldwide superstardom? The writing of "Crime Wave," of course – the middle that remains missing, even within this fantasy space, the thing that Steven *cannot even imagine* and so could never accomplish.

The Final Failure

Steven Penny's wild fantasies continue to falter, fail, and make way for more elaborate versions, phoenix-like in their perpetual rebirth. As these hyperreal birds die and are reborn every few seconds, before our very eyes, the dream/film's bizarre propulsion continues. While "Steven" crouches over his typewriter, the lights go out, just as they did when he was a child. Not just in his room, but in the cityscape outside his window, the lights die and the soundtrack dies with them. Instead of the monstrous voice from his childhood, silence reigns. Jesus himself appears from the shadows. But even this strange achievement, being singled out by God, does not satisfy. No, next, we see "Steven" stepping into the role of Jesus, as if becoming a god. He washes the feet of the prisoner Jolly, the Judas scriptwriter whose betrayal has been to teach

Steven the importance of "twists," that Hollywood narrative cure-all. Although we're told by the narrator that this experience finally seems to satisfy "Steven," we know not to trust the narrator, and know too that "Steven" will go on to type his final apology. As Jolly and "Steven" hug, Jolly glides hands down to cup the Christ-like filmmaker's buttocks, undercutting any accidental sentimentality in this "forgiveness" scene.

Like any self-respecting theme park mogul, "Steven" is "frozen for the ages." A funeral procession pays its respects, and although he has died, in true "Crime Wave" fashion his legacy lives on. The narrator recalls, quizzically, the last words typewritten by this silent God in his death throes: "'I real ly did mean to be good.' Well, Steven, if you were alive today, I wonder what you'd say to these kids, the hope of the future, who really do mean to be just like you." The narrator delivers the phrase "just like you" in threatening tones, to a dramatic swell of discordant music, as if uttering a threat. This narrator remains oblivious to the disparity between how his words and tone relate to the images and scenes he narrates (as he does throughout the other incarnations of "Crime Wave"). By contrast, in this final beginning and ending, screenwriter Steven Penny at last seems self-aware. The narrator announces triumph, and both Kim and the manifest content of *Crime Wave* echo the narrator in regarding this final beginning and ending as a victory. However, with the typed apology, "Steven" makes explicit an admission of failure that is otherwise only implied. The finale of the Steven–Kim plot likewise mixes triumphant joy with an ironic undercurrent of despair and violence. Kim wakes to find Steven passed out on the typewriter, street light disappeared, head still bloody. Kim reads over Steven's shoulder as he wakes. The two hold the same pose as the young children (who want to be "just like" Steven) from the final moments of the last "Crime Wave" ending. This matched pose, like Steven's connection to Lyle and his friendship with Kim, invites us to view Steven as a man-child, immature and unsophisticated, without the conscious self-awareness that his written self has just displayed.

Žižek notes that "even when the subject himself appears within his narrative, this is not automatically his point of identification – that is, he by no means necessarily 'identifies with himself.'"[15] Since the "Steven Penny" inside the fantasy frame finds himself disillusioned with his apparent success, we might (by contrast) see Steven-as-author identifying himself, to some degree, with his double in the narrative (this is the basis for interpreting the typewritten apology as an apology). We should note, however, the change in Steven's own subjective position relative to how he appears in the framing story. Creating and situating his double and his/its "apology" within the fantasy frame serves as a distancing technique, so that Steven effectively relates to himself as an "Other" through the mechanism of the fantasy. This allows Steven, after he awakens, to read through his final beginning and ending with Kim and smile. Along with everyone else, Steven rejoices in having finally produced a workable beginning and ending, instead of discarding this one too. Yet, as the typewritten last words indicate, this beginning and ending should only be "final" in the sense that he has finally lost all hope and recognized his absolute failure, as the "last words" of this quiet man reveal. What has forestalled this recognition?

It's as if, somewhere in the missing middle, Steven entered into his script (to become the fictitious "Steven Penny" that recognizes his failure with these "last words"), trading places with his double, who entered into the "reality" frame diegesis to enjoy the illusory success. Steven Penny *after* this final beginning and ending seems closer to the oblivious narrator he created than the "Steven Penny" *in* this final ending, who seems closer to *us* – the distanced viewers who observe Steven's final beginning and ending with ironic detachment. We are, after being held at a distance, now close to him, and so in a position to understand the film-within-a-film "Steven Penny" better than the Steven Penny of

Crime Wave's core/frame narrative. These "last words" can be read as the only moment in the film where he truly "speaks" to us, where irony suspends itself and we get a direct statement of sorrow, all the more heartbreaking for being an apology. As a result, it is easy to forget that it is Steven's *double* who apologizes, his fantasy self, since this phantasmatic "Steven" seems *more real* than the supposedly "real" Steven doing the fantasizing. The very fact of his apparent "reality" – that he is suddenly a fully realized character with depth – should be taken as the surest sign of the double's phantasmatic identity. Steven approaches the core of his fantasy and discovers its impossible kernel (that the creation of "Crime Wave" will always elude him), and this threatens the collapse of his fantasy and the concomitant dissolution of "reality." Yet Steven returns to this "reality" of the narrative frame story – *Crime Wave* does not "end" within this ending. More precisely, Steven retreats from the film-within-a-film fantasy outward to a fuller, more stable, exaggerated version of this fantasy: rather than imagining that he will one day craft the "greatest color crime movie ever made" by producing the script for "Crime Wave," Steven now imagines that he *has already done so* by producing (alongside Kim) the script for John Paizs's *Crime Wave*. His initial disavowal of the impossibility of writing "Crime Wave" spurred forth the fantasy of its possibility, but by now Steven has traversed his fantasy, and rather than accepting its impossible kernel, he retreats from the realization by foreclosing that realization more drastically (he won't "one day" write "Crime Wave" – he has *already* written it, even though he *still* cannot write middles). Steven's traumatic encounter with the core of his fantasy, in other words, has resulted in psychotic withdrawal.

A Happy/Hollywood Ending?

Kim loves this new ending, and even her parents smile and laugh as they read. The trash cans collect only snow. Although Steven has not learned to write middles, Kim has: "I've got one right here and it's all about Steven's struggle, and you just saw most of it." This raises the possibility that Steven and Kim have collaborated to produce John Paizs's *Crime Wave,* as noted above; it also suggests that all of the bizarre plot twists in the latter part of the film were of Kim's invention (again, a Donald Kaufman-esque taking of the screenplay's reins), which perhaps explains their absurdity. The unbelievable "twist" that Kim could possibly have any idea how to write acceptable middles further supports the idea that this ending should be read as phantasmatic. Kim's next proclamation, that the two of them will "make it to the top and cut everything right down the middle," does not seem that it will settle well with the Steven Penny whose megalomaniacal fantasies we've just glimpsed. As she calls to him for confirmation ("Right, Steven?") he stands in the kitchen, unresponsive, sharpening a knife.

Kim continues to call to Steven, and he begins to advance on her, knife held behind his back. The tone shifts again, as in the meeting with Dr Jolly, to one of threat. Steven thrusts out towards her – but he's now holding a celebratory cake, the pyramid-shaped globe cake from each of his early beginnings of "Crime Wave." He uses the sharpened knife to cut it, "right down the middle" like Kim said, and they stuff their faces playfully. The original scripted scene offers a similar but darker version of these events: Steven "raises a kitchen knife and motions to Kim not to move ... Steven looms over her. His shadow goes up her face. Suddenly he stabs. Kim screams. The knife goes into a rat that was sneaking up behind Kim."[16]

What's startling about Paizs's deft moves into and out of the dark undercurrent of his film, in moments like these, is how the shift to darkness seems natural, but the return to light-hearted comedy does not negate this revealed darkness. Steven would clearly resent Kim's ability to write middles, since it emphasizes his own failure, and would be reluctant to let her in on his dream. His resentment would naturally

Kim Brown (Eva Kovacs) – writing to Dr Jolly, or writing "Crime Wave"? Courtesy of John Paizs, from the director's personal collection.

develop into the kind of murderous jealousy typical of the color crime movie genre (especially in the original script, with its mock-murder of Kim with the prop knife). But Kim's just a little girl, and his only real friend, so why not laugh and have a piece of cake? Perhaps we can read this final "twist" as personal growth – as Steven putting his dreams of color crime movie superstardom to rest and sharing the glory with Kim, to produce the artful *Crime Wave*. Since this is "A Favorite Pictures Production" and not "A Steven Penny Production," we might read the final title card as affirming this personal growth, but it would be more consistent with the film's trajectory to instead view these plot developments as Steven losing all self-awareness and entering into a state of total delusion.

The ending music also cues us to accept Steven and Kim's partnership as positive and productive, although its excessive nature marks this cueing as ironic. The cheerful music that accompanied the film's lightest moments returns now, bolstered with saccharine lyrics (by George Toles, best known as author of the ironic, melodramatic dialogue of Maddin's movies). The song confirms this happy ending and suggests the marriage that is traditional to the final act of comedies:

Steven and Kim are buddies
Also partners in life
Maybe when Kim has grown up
They'll even be husband and wife
When street lights glow in the evening
And lawmen do as they should
Steven and Kim are typing
Stories to make us feel good

Middles are hard to think of
As every scriptwriter knows

Steven would often panic
Go rigid right down to his toes
Now he has Kim to help him
There's barely a cloud in the sky
Steven is almost happy
As sane as you or I

This second verse repeats, so that the film ends with this strange declaration that Steven is "almost happy" (his happiness must be qualified!) and "as sane as you or I." This aggressive insistence counteracts the possibility of personal growth that the "happy ending" appears to offer.

We should return to the notion of "normality" offered by McGowan to explain the work of David Lynch, discussed above with reference to Dr Jolly. In the scene where Steven "forgave" Jolly by washing his feet, the walls of Jolly's cell were plastered with photos of male bodies in sexual poses; they were similar, then, to the walls of Billy Botski's home (decorated with "Connies") or of Steven's own garage apartment (plastered with color crime movie posters). Jolly and Steven were already connected, as screenwriters, but the set design strengthens this connection and further links Jolly to the "quiet man" figure, associating the abnormal "quiet man" with madness. Žižek notes that "madness [is] the positive foundation of 'normality': it is not madness which is a secondary and accidental distortion of normality; rather, it is normality itself which is nothing but gentrified/regulated madness."[17] Steven has embraced his insanity, but the narrative structure of *Crime Wave*, its metafictional apparatus, succeeds in "regulating" this madness to produce a parody of the "happy" Hollywood ending.

By now, it is apparent that the true object of *Crime Wave*'s title, the true subject of the film, is the "Crime Wave" *that does not exist* – the one that Steven Penny has failed, and will always fail, to produce. The very existence of John Paizs's *Crime Wave* makes Steven's "Crime Wave" both potential (because it is imagined) and impossible (because it is displaced). Even in this cheerful ending, the darkness will not abate. Earnest professions of Steven's sanity in this irony-soaked film cannot but be read as the opposite – as confirmation that this quiet man is quite insane.

7

An Alternate Universe

A different ending for *Crime Wave* exists. Although not uncommon in Hollywood film, alternate endings are rare among cash-strapped productions. Still more rare, Paizs's decision to reconceptualize, rewrite, and reshoot *Crime Wave*'s ending occurred *after* the film's festival premiere. This decision cost Paizs not just time and money but momentum. Pevere speculates on whether there might have been

> some alternative-universe future for *Crime Wave*. Where things might have turned out differently *if*: *if* the movie hadn't broken down when it did; *if* Paizs hadn't taken over a year to re-shoot the ending of an already-finished movie [in fact, Paizs premiered the re-shot ending within half a year – Pevere must base his timeline on the film's home video release]; *if* he'd been able to maintain the momentum that *might* have been built if the movie had vaulted from a stunning festival premiere to a still buzzing commercial opening.
>
> But those *ifs* are like Steven's middles: purely speculative, easy to ponder and finally beyond practical use. The fact is, the movie (which actually received some stunning reviews) disappeared for a year only to return in significantly altered form – the one we still have – at a point when interest had waned, the press was looking elsewhere and the prospect of anything other than a nominal theatrical life was impossible. It didn't

> matter that the new *Crime Wave* was arguably improved. By the time it returned, the audience had gone home.[1]

The original version of the film is even less available than its now-unavailable final version (which was at least released to home video on VHS). It is perhaps too easy to emulate the imaginary members of Steven's "Crime Wave" club, and wring hands over "what might have been." In so doing, we contribute to an image of Paizs as a naïf like Penny, with a perfectionist streak, who simply did not realize that he was dooming his film by withdrawing it from circulation following its premiere. Perhaps we should vindicate Paizs, instead, as an uncompromising auteur. Paizs's new ending to *Crime Wave* is not just "arguably improved" but masterful. The finished ending to *Crime Wave* replaces an original ending that, despite moments of brilliance, possesses severe structural flaws. Would another director have been able, even with the help of reviewers, to sense precisely how this otherwise successful film had failed?

Into a Middle

Although Paizs made a number of changes throughout *Crime Wave* before settling on its final form, Pevere notes correctly that only the ending was "significantly altered." The significant differences between the original and final endings begin as Steven advances along the government fence in Kansas towards his meeting with Dr Jolly. Steven comes across some trucks parked along the fence, with young children playing nearby. The government agents in yellow jumpsuits warn them all away. As Steven nears, everyone grows still. They seem to stare at Steven, motionless as startled deer. Even a dog stops to stare. And then, without a word, they unfreeze and return to their playing. In fact, the children have responded not to Steven but to distant gunshots. However, the editing and the suddenness of their shifts from playing to staring tinge the scene, as if they see something in Steven that disturbs them more than these echoed executions.

The scene grows stranger. Steven realizes that he is standing beside a billboard emblazoned with only the word *and*. Scanning the Kansas fields, he discovers other billboards in a presumed series, which no doubt contain the remaining words of some sentence. But the other billboards either face away from him or are too faded to read. Steven is left to puzzle out this *and* – a conjunction – by definition the "middle" of some sentence. Steven lacks – in a sudden reversal of his fortunes that signals a shift from the film-before-now – a beginning and an end. He has found himself inside of some middle. Pevere's complaint that, in the original ending, it seems that some other film has taken the place of *Crime Wave* does a nice job of describing the shift in tone. In another "twist," Steven finds himself inside a middle that seems to belong to some new movie altogether, but his assimilation into this new narrative cannot be completed. This failure to incorporate the Kansas sequence in *Crime Wave* is in a sense the subject of the Kansas story, whose characters will eventually get fed up with Steven and kick him out – taunting Steven that he needs to get back to (the writing of) his own story.

Eerily, the billboard's *and* can also be read as the film's unconscious admission of this original ending's flaws. Paizs has by now abandoned the film-within-a-film structure – a structure that, according to the narrative logic of Steven's storyline, should culminate in his writing of a final beginning and ending to "Crime Wave." In this original ending, by comparison, the established narrative logic falters. After undergoing adventures in Kansas, Steven returns to Winnipeg a changed man. We neither see him write another beginning and ending nor view it for ourselves, although we are told that Steven has nevertheless completed his script (it's suggested that *Crime Wave*'s script is the one that Steven completes). The billboard's *and* seems to point to this lack: Where is the rest of the sentence? Where is the final film-within-a-film beginning and ending that *Crime Wave*'s structure has implicitly promised?

We can also read this *and*, in its fragmentary meaninglessness, as a pointedly postmodern gesture within a film that draws together such gestures without granting them meaning through this cohesion. The weakness of *Crime Wave*'s original ending is that the film's postmodernism here reaches an early climax. Past this point, *Crime Wave* devolves into simple parody and empty nostalgia, rather than the complex pastiche and complicated irony that, as noted above, Jameson and Hutcheon have identified as hallmarks of postmodern art. In the original ending of *Crime Wave*, Steven does not approach and violently withdraw from the traumatic kernel of his fantasy: instead he discovers (like Dorothy) that he had the ability to write "Crime Wave" all along. Steven only needs to give up his self-doubt to realize his fantasy, in a happy ending without the dark undercurrent that Paizs layers into the revised ending of the film's finished version.

The Displacement of Steven Penny

The betrayal of *Crime Wave*'s narrative and structural logic continues as Steven, our "quiet man," speaks. An old woman, "Mother," who piggybacks on the mentally challenged Ethan, approaches Steven and asks if this is his first time visiting Kansas. "Yes, it is," he replies. This is the only instance in the film when Steven speaks a line directly, on-screen. That it is such a banal line, with no possible weight, signals this moment as an *über*-postmodern gesture: self-conscious artistic suicide. Paizs has by now thrown away all of the film's central conceits, and signalled within the film that he has done so. Mother's response confirms this: "Oh, a quiet man, eh?" She labels him quiet, echoing Kim, even though she knows nothing of his silence. Steven has just spoken to her, after all,

John Paizs and Mark Yuill filming an "animal ad racket" scene later cut from *Crime Wave*. Courtesy of John Paizs, from the director's personal collection.

and has even added a superfluous "it is" after his "yes" – for Steven, this is positively chatty. Ethan leaves Mother with Steven and heads off to collect empty bottles from the field. The children torment Ethan, who drops the bottles as the brats pile upon him. Mother upbraids Ethan – "You don't take that no more" – and Ethan apologizes for dropping the bottles. The two come across like Warner Bros. cartoon versions of John Steinbeck characters. Their bizarre caricatures soar above any of the absurdity we've seen so far, but lack the dimension of threat or darkness present in Paizs's other stock characters. They are "copies" of another sort – more in line with the ironic approach that Hutcheon praises in conventional postmodern parody, and thus less complicated than the rest of Paizs's copying.

Mother and Ethan leave, and Steven continues along the fence, stopping for the night and donning his sweater, then crouching and eating his licorice, as in the final version of the scene. Dr Jolly arrives, and his meeting with Steven plays out the same way, for the most part. Jolly does add a creepy but effective line that "maybe Kansas just makes people look different than they are," which reflects on the apparent unreality of this dream-like Kansas. However, in this ending, although the scene is quite similar to its final version, Dr Jolly seems less threatening. To some degree his lack of threat results from the scene playing longer and being sillier. Also, prior to this scene, with Mother and Ethan, Kansas was established as a cartoonish realm, so Jolly is just another cartoon. Even in moments otherwise identical to those of the finished version, he lacks occasional menace because of this different context. Stranger still, when Steven runs away, Dr Jolly collapses for no apparent reason instead of following. After a long pause, Steven returns as if concerned for the murderous doctor he has just fled. There's blood on the back of Jolly's head – Ethan has knocked out Jolly with a bottle. (We later learn that Jolly had attempted to "mount" Ethan.) Before we discover any of this, some hillbillies appear, disfigured from the "secret stuff," and strike Steven with their truck in their flight from unseen government agents. Ethan rescues Steven again, carrying him to the ramshackle home he shares with Mother. (Ethan is played by Mitch Funk, of the punk band Personality Crisis, which was the subject of the 2008 book *Personality Crisis: Warm Beer and Wild Times*, by Chris Walter. As with Angela Heck, a bit player in *Crime Wave* who later became known from her appearances in Guy Maddin's films, particularly her role as Snjófridur in *Tales from the Gimli Hospital*, the presence of Funk in *Crime Wave* suggests the degree to which Paizs was able to command the respect and cooperation of then-important figures in various Winnipeg arts scenes.)

By this point, Ethan and Mother have displaced Steven as the film's active figures. The original ending of *Crime Wave* thereby hews closer to the typical formula of Canadian cinema, where a passive protagonist gets swept along by more active figures (here, a Canadian caught up with Americans), although in other respects it can hardly be said that *Crime Wave* follows the conventions of Canadian cinema. In any case, Mother and Ethan displace Steven as the stars of *Crime Wave*'s ending, in contrast to the operation of the finished film, in which Steven falls deeper "into" *Crime Wave* by becoming the star of "Crime Wave." Mother will later make this very point – that Steven has become too passive and reliant on her in the same way that Ethan has (she noted when Steven met her that Ethan wasn't her son, and when she sends Steven away she will remark that she doesn't need a second "son").

The police come to Mother's the next day to investigate; having arrested Jolly, they are on the lookout for Steven. Mother pleads ignorance, covering for Steven. She later informs Steven that he can stay with them if he likes. Mother soon rescinds this offer, after regarding Steven's attempts to help out around the shack with increasing annoyance. Paizs conveys Steven's brief taste of the simple life with a bundle of comically banal clichés – he chops wood, they fry fresh-caught fish over an open fire, and Mother reads Ethan and Steven to sleep from the Book of Lamentations. The last straw comes when Steven snuggles up in bed with Mother and Ethan. Mother has already reported that she resents Ethan's child-like attentions, and seems to resent Steven's even more. Steven wakes in the night to find Mother leaning over him, Ethan cavorting in the background. Rationalizing that Steven likes crime, Mother tells him, "I'm gonna show you a crime so revolting and so shameful you won't believe it once you've seen it." The tone darkens, but the film cannot commit to this shift. We have left the inventive landscape of *Crime Wave* for a realm of movie-of-the-week cliché where nothing attracts our attention for long. Steven seems to have given up writing "Crime Wave," given up on his desire, in favour of a new fantasy (without clear relation to the previous narrative arc): being able to live an "authentic" life through abandonment of art(ifice) and "return" to the (American heart)land.

The Sense of Non-Ending

Mother and Ethan lead Steven to the water's edge, force him to face his reflection in the water, then kick him into the darkness with a splash. "Finish what you started," Mother counsels as Ethan chases Steven away with thrown bottles. Why a woman living in a backwoods shack should care about whether or not Steven finishes his screenplay is unclear, but more pressing is that her pragmatic home remedy reduces Steven's writer's block to a species of laziness. However true this might be in reality (I had to drag myself from the couch to write this sentence), the equation of writer's block with laziness within the film's world simplifies the impossibility of Steven ever creating "Crime Wave" – now it is entirely possible, even inevitable. The fundamental lack that at once demands, sustains, and threatens the fantasy that Steven uses to "create" himself turns into a character flaw that, once realized, can be overcome. After Steven stumbles across a bus and returns to Canada, Kim reinforces this idea: now, "'Crime Wave' is going just fine. Steven thought of a way to stuff most of his old ideas between an all-new beginning and ending, and that isn't so much trouble." This resolution still nods to *Crime Wave*'s metafictional structure, but does not return to that structure (we do not get to see any new "stuff" from Steven's reimagined "Crime Wave"), and Kim's place within this larger structure is unclear. *Crime Wave* no longer knows what to do with Kim once Steven leaves for Kansas. She disappears from the film, as both a character and a narrator, from the time Steven leaves Winnipeg until its final scene, where she repeats Mother's actions, placing a mirror on the floor so that Steven sees his own face when he bends over and she can kick him in the butt. In this way, Kim says, she tries "to encourage [Steven] whenever I can."

In the *Globe and Mail* review of the film that led Paizs to reconsider this ending, Jay Scott isolates the particular problem of this original ending: "The premise until then, a parody of the creative process, is betrayed in favor of picaresque misadventures crazed enough to be the work of [John] Waters, but without the requisite bravado. More important, they are not funny enough to hold boredom at bay."[2] The problem in fact goes further than this, because *Crime Wave* is not just a "parody of the creative process" but a film that presents the creative process as a slow march unto death. The production of narrative presents itself as the construction of fantasy that enables the creation of reality, along with anxiety about the fragility of these structures. By betraying the film's established edifice, *Crime Wave*'s original ending also devolves into greeting-card sentimentality. We might view the scenes with Ethan and Mother as satirical, as poking fun at the easy answers offered by so many "happy endings," but the film nevertheless produces these same answers, however ironically. Žižek neatly locates the emptiness of such gestures: "Instead of praising these displacements and reinscriptions

Dave Peter helps prepare John Paizs who, as Steven Penny, prepares to teach Kim about squibs in a scene later cut from *Crime Wave*. Courtesy of John Paizs, from the director's personal collection.

too readily as potentially 'subversive' ... we should focus on the obvious fact that, through all these displacements, *the same old story is being told*. In short, the true function of these displacements and subversions is precisely to make the traditional story relevant to our 'postmodern' age – and thus to prevent us from replacing it with a new narrative."[3]

Along these lines, the original ending of *Crime Wave* seems almost Puritan in its final message: if Steven had just rolled up his sleeves and gotten down to the hard work of writing "Crime Wave" in the first place, he would not have wasted all this time and gotten himself into this trouble with Dr Jolly. (Of course, then Paizs also wouldn't have a problem around which to structure *Crime Wave*'s plot.) Most discordant, Mother's home recipe for writer's block, a kick in the butt, echoes Brock's complaint in *Oak, Ivy, and Other Dead Elms*: "What this country needs is a good old-fashioned kick in the pants." *Oak* presents Brock as a nostalgic dictator with delusions of grandeur, so how should we read the same sentiment – no longer a doomed wish, but advice that works – coming from the mouth of Mother? And echoed by Kim? As a non-answer, perhaps, but that would make this a non-ending. More to the point, Steven just needing a "kick" defuses and dismisses his felt anxiety (since "Crime Wave" goes fine once he gets the kick), and the preservation of this anxiety is central to *Crime Wave*. Rather than an ambivalent film that views the absence of any stable, non-fantasized reality as a necessary, painful, postmodern "truth," this original ending assumes the existence of an authentic world as locatable, if Steven would just stop living in his fantasies and remove them to their proper place (a script held as a created world apart from him).

I criticize this original ending of *Crime Wave* in order to praise Paizs for his acknowledgment of the film's problems, a realization that went beyond the mild negativity of its reviews. Scott complained of the film's increasing craziness, and audiences responded negatively to its shift into a darker register, yet Paizs chose not to downplay but to *extend* these elements. In its finished form, the film's craziness reaches new heights ("How about a theme park!") and grows ever darker through maintaining and deepening Steven's anxieties. It cannot be known whether or not Paizs's decision to reshoot the film's ending squandered its commercial potential, since we have cause to suspect the commercial potential of a bizarre postmodern metafiction in the first place, never mind a Canadian one. More certain is the rightness of Paizs's decision on artistic grounds. The finished version of the film, ending as it does, is an undeniable improvement over its original version. Would *Crime Wave* had survived so long, against all odds, and attracted its cult in this original form? Perhaps, but it would certainly not be the subject of this book, since it would not return in Steven's final beginning and ending to raise self-critical questions about Steven's impossible desires. The triumph of *Crime Wave*, in its final form, is that it's a postmodernist work that steps away to regard its postmodernism, from a distance, with horror. This tension complicates a now-staid metafictional plot device (the writer as character in his own production). Although "the 'blocked filmmaker'/'film about making a film' genre has taken off since ... the mid-80s [when] it was still wide open for exploration,"[4] *Crime Wave* develops tropes established by earlier films like Fellini's *8½* (1963) while anticipating yet avoiding the dead ends of later, more simplistic, self-reflexive films. The final beginning and ending of the finished *Crime Wave* anchors Steven's anxiety through his seeming self-awareness (and its subsequent total disavowal), complicates the film's already strained distinction between reality and fantasy, and suggests tensions between American and Canadian cinema. *Crime Wave* thereby revolves around Steven's anxious realization of the impossibility of crafting authentic, meaningful art within a cultural industry – a term that has become an oxymoron. Although we can no longer find culture apart from industry, because that industry is American we cannot produce culture, only its cold simulacrum.

8

From the North

Steven Penny arrives "from the North" (i.e., from Canada) to crush the old order and forge a new color crime movie empire. For he has a dream: to create the greatest color crime movie ever made. But note the dimensions of this dream. He dreams in colour, our Steven. No stark blacks and whites, no *film noir* grimness will accompany his criminal visions. We can expect Steven's "Crime Wave" to be as brightly saturated as Paizs's own *Crime Wave*. Kim suggests at the film's end that we have just watched either Steven's "Crime Wave" or a "making-of" documentary whose sequel will be the real "Crime Wave." But the film we've just watched is a comedy. And we see no sequel. In a tragic real-world twist, Paizs will not write and direct another film after *Crime Wave*.

Steven intends to make a crime movie focusing (if we are to judge by his failed beginnings and endings) on the rise and fall of criminal celebrities who, despite their reprehensible actions, remain inspirational for all long after their final, fatal runs from the police. As protagonists, Steven offers some modern-day desperadoes. Steven's ambition is tremendous: his film will stand and be recognized as the undeniable pinnacle of color crime movie achievement. In short, Steven Penny wants to make an American movie, shot in C-O-L-O-R.

What lies at the heart of this dream, drives it forward? Sheer love of cinema, of the color crime movie genre? The thrill of creation, some need for artistic expression? Perhaps in part, but Steven shares the tragic flaw of his protagonists. His desire to be the best – for fame – forestalls his work, prevents the perfection of his talent. His need for recognition, to make his mark on the culture – and on the American film industry, on Hollywood – prevents his personal and even his artistic growth. He's too full of anxiety, a Bloomian anxiety of influence – even the films he produces in his fantasies are derivative of Hollywood movies. His very fantasies themselves appear derivative, copies of copies, packed with clichés and theme parks. His imagination, from the outset, shows the marks of its colonization. The American fantasy of the individual free to engage in the "pursuit of happiness" is itself a dream of "limitless increase" (in Baudrillard's sense of a compulsion without goal, possessing neither ethics nor the possibility of satisfaction). Steven displays this same desperation to enjoy when faced with his dissolving fantasy, and the narrative structure of his final scripted ending to "Crime Wave" details his own failing "pursuit of happiness."

Steven's desperation arises from two main frustrations. The first is that he is unable to write middles, a necessity when attempting to craft the greatest color crime movie script ever (an unfortunate precondition for creating the greatest color crime movie ever). The second is that he has betrayed his dream from its conception, by desiring not so much its fulfilment as the recognition of that fulfilment. Steven longs for the attendant celebrity more than for the dream itself. This self-betrayal, and its recognition in the womb, may be the cause of Steven's strange strain of writer's block. He's obsessed with "endings" – end results – with success and celebrity, but he is also stuck in a "beginning" – far from realizing these dreams. He sees no way to close the distance between the achievement of his dreams and their initial stirrings, cannot focus on the necessary "middles." How could he?

The ultimate irony of *Crime Wave* is that Steven Penny fails to produce a film like John Paizs's *Crime Wave*. He's a quiet man, without American confidence to match his American ambition. How could he ever marshal the will to finish his screenplay? Or the resources to produce his movie? How can he "break in" to the Hollywood "racket" if he comes "from the North"? Even worse, from Winnipeg? He can only dream his way to success. Through Steven's lame dream of becoming a Hollywood schlockmeister, Paizs satirizes what Tom McSorley calls "the persistent attitude towards filmmaking in Canada that favours the production of imitations of American-style films to achieve commercial success."[1] Steven's final beginning and ending reimagines his dream to create the greatest color crime movie ever as a virulent strain of manifest destiny.

Do we go too far in suggesting that Steven Penny might stand in, metaphorically, for a Canadian film industry overshadowed by the American film industry? For a national cinema confronted by its own creative blocks, producing pathetic derivative works even when it really does mean to be good? Obviously, Canada has produced excellent films, works of great artistry and originality (as *Crime Wave* itself attests). Nevertheless, the most common criticism levelled at Canadian cinema, and its most obvious flaw, is that it has too often failed to step out from the shadow of American influence – that its imagination has been colonized, just like Steven's. But how can one step out from that shadow? Is this possible, or even desirable? Such anxiety has come to be seen as a hallmark of Canadian identity (or attempts at identity), due to Canada's geographical, cultural, and economic proximity to the United States. As Jameson notes, "[Canada is] fully exposed to the unprotected blasts of the mass culture which is one of the fundamental exports of the United States and which Canada is under constant pressure to admit and be submerged by."[2]

The question of Canadian identity was an "old question" even in 1980, when Anthony Wilden wrote that "because Canada is a neocolony of the United States, there is no truly international relationship between the people of Canada and the people of the United States."[3]

Instead, to couch the matter in psychoanalytic terms, there is a paranoiac relationship between the two, where Canadians see their lack of identity *as* an identity of sorts, (un)developed due to neocolonial attention from the American Other (whose proximity prevents our enjoyment of ourselves). Wilden argued that "Canadians are brought up in the home and in the school in a tissue of contradictions about American people, American capital, and supposedly 'American' ideas. Too often these contradictions involve an introverted feeling of inferiority to the American giant ... This is felt and experienced as violence. But recognizing the real source of this violence is dangerous; and attempting to turn it back on its actual sources is psychological suicide."[4] In this view, Steven's obsession with violence seems appropriate, as does his difficulty sustaining an identity in/through his fantasies of success.

Linda Hutcheon, in *Splitting Images*, her examination of how irony plays a fundamental role in a postmodern conception of Canadian identity, quotes Margaret Atwood's own claim: Canadians, according to Atwood, were "doing the same old Canadian tango, which is: do we exist? don't we exist? – except that we have gone round a couple of more times. We've established the fact of our own existence and now we are prepared to abolish ourselves."[5] The situation of Steven Penny is precisely reversed. He has "gone round" enough to know that he will never write "Crime Wave," but as the protagonist of *Crime Wave* his failure threatens to annul his own metafictional existence. He struggles to maintain the failing fantasy that guarantees his anxious identity, in a desperate attempt to believe in the power of "a dream."

The Canadian Pursuit of Failure

Concerning the experience of first viewing Paizs's films, Pevere declares that "for what felt like the first time in my life, I was watching Canadian films that reflected the Canada I had grown up in ... Not the Canada that had been imposed on me since infancy, but the one in which I actually lived. A country where one spent one's life watching TV imported from somewhere else, and where irony – as embodied most dramatically by Paizs's own deadpan presence on screen – was not so much a presumed attitude as an unavoidable state of being."[6] Paizs's irony is a special brand of postmodern irony, a just-as-"unavoidable" side effect of this postmodern "state of being." (Matthew Rankin, another filmmaker bearing the influence of Paizs – most apparent in his work with the loose filmmaking collective L'Atelier National du Manitoba – regards this "state of being" as typical of Paizs's hometown: "Winnipeg is not a city, it is a form of irony.")[7] Rather than attempt to recuperate some authentic experience, or some essential identity, *Crime Wave* assumes the disconnect from any meaningful or sensible reality as the very basis for any such identity: an identity so disconnected from its contextual reality that it can be transported from filmed world to filmed world.

For all its humour, Paizs's stance self-reflexively treats this ironic position as one worthy of anxious philosophical reflection and introspection. It does so rather than celebrating, as Hutcheon does, and thereby "[making] a virtue"[8] of an ironic identity. In doing so, "[Paizs] speaks to that vast generation of culturally polluted schizophrenic Canadians ... for whom television was a persistently seductive, and ultimately masochistic, vision of what we wished for but could never attain: to be just like our Older brother [the United States]."[9] Rather than attempt to step out from the American shadow, and avoid U.S. influence, Paizs through his irony occupies a position that is ambivalent about even its own ambivalence. Pevere further notes that "*Crime Wave* may be the first Canadian movie that addresses the perennial issue and phenomenon of American media saturation in Canada that does not take absolute sides ... but instead acknowledges the actual complexity of the Canadian obsession ... with our big brother's ceaseless northwards popculture onslaught."[10] Paizs's artistic strategy of "copying" produces, as an effect, the film's implicit argument that the forging of a unique cultural identity in the face of American globalism is a fool's errand. After postmodernism, any attempt to forge a national identity must avoid an unrealistic and unsustainable essentialism by acknowledging the impossibility of a stable identity in the process of its self-creation, rather than taking *any* virtue (even the "virtue" of irony) as its constitutive kernel.

Running towards the U.S. giant constitutes a failure of the national imagination. So does running from it. Instead, we should accept, absorb, and creatively repackage – copy – that influence in a strange bid to exert some control. In an interview with Mark Peranson, Paizs asks: "Is there a Canadian culture that is distinct to begin with? Certainly in my life, growing up, I never watched whatever there was supposed to be Canadian ... I completely unselfconsciously took and absorbed everything from the States. It never worried me."[11] Steven, by contrast, worries. In Steven's failure, which is Paizs's triumph, *Crime Wave* implies an ironic solution to Canadian anxiety over the lack of a stable identity: accept this anxiety as a productive state of being. This is how Paizs succeeds where Penny fails. Steven cannot escape the "order," much less "smash" it, so his imagined success on U.S. terms does not satisfy. But Paizs embraces the order to realize Penny's dreams, to produce the *Crime Wave* that Steven cannot. As Pevere writes: "In Paizs' hands ... the pop culturated world [is] absorbed and regurgitated without being trivialized or trashed. Ironically, there's something almost reverent in Paizs' painstaking, virtually hand-made mashups of his boomerized junk-culture background, a kind of outsider-art appreciation that sanctifies by simple virtue of such single-minded dedication."[12]

Steven Penny lacks this single-mindedness. With Steven's last words in the final beginning and ending of "Crime Wave," he indicts himself and apologizes for the un-Canadian extravagance of his desires. Steven seems aware, now, that his hunger for fame does not express a longing to be integrated into the larger social order, from which he is isolated due to being a "quiet man" in a world of talkers, an artist whose work has personal importance but cannot hold public interest, and a Canadian who is invisible beside that behemoth to the south. Steven wants to smash the order but can only bow to it (since such aggression is a form of acquiescence), and this leads to his dissatisfaction even with dreamed success. Living in imposed anonymity due to his suburban, urban, national, and international invisibility, Steven desires not mere recognition in these various social spheres, but to establish a sort of revengeful dominance. He wants to outshine his Canadian neighbours and out-American the American ones. To do so, he is not averse to playing by Dr Jolly's screenwriting rules. Having realized his ability to compromise his (imagined) artistry, Steven apologizes with his last words for the part he has played – in his fantasies if nowhere else – in sustaining and spurring forward the American/Hollywood juggernaut.

If, as Pevere has suggested, "*Crime Wave*'s world is one where the media, its consumers and its effects are indistinguishable,"[13] then it is the American media, its Canadian consumers, and its effects of instilling endless desire for cultural forcefulness alongside the realization of exclusion from this origin of cultural power. Paizs, although he may stand, "ironically enough ... as our most American filmmaker,"[14] is no Penny. Guy Maddin, self-described "cub reporter," argues that "[*Crime Wave*] is definitely Canadian ... but it is not Canadian in the way we are used to our movies being. It does not attempt to lyricize the acts of plunging your arms into prairie soil or getting drunk in the Ontario Northwest. *Crime Wave* is nationalistic ... foremost, by having at its centre a strange mental world, not a geographical one."[15] Alongside this notion, we might consider Pevere's sense that "being Canadian might mean enduring a condition of acute cultural alienation and inferiority, but being Canadian like John Paizs means turning that condition into a strategy for assaulting the dominant media and turning trash into something resembling art."[16] At the heart of Paizs's postmodern aesthetic is a process of copying that may appear to be haphazard pastiche but has the rigour of modernist collage. This refusal to adopt a slavish adherence to any artistic camp, or even to the identity politics that underlie "camp," in favour of the dogged pursuit of a comic vision, is what allows Paizs's work to tower above more recent exercises in postmodern self-reflexivity. *Crime Wave* is not a hermetic, sealed puzzle of a film, nor is it a film that refers endlessly outward.

Paizs's triumph in *Crime Wave* is that he has disconnected the postmodern from its -ism. *Crime Wave* flaunts a postmodern aesthetic but does not reduce itself to a series of gestures or surfaces, nor does it retreat to a stable, nostalgic position of longing for ideologies past. *Crime Wave* instead displays a profound anxiety about the status of reality, but it embraces this anxiety as the basis for both continual processes of identity production and a black, ironic joy. Hutcheon writes that "irony itself inherently undercuts [pretensions to master narratives] and the postmodern irony of today does so consciously."[17] However, the postmodern indictment of master narratives operates unconsciously as a master narrative within postmodernism, as its ironic organizing principle and originating mythology. For this reason, the work of a figure like Žižek, who remains a harsh critic of postmodern thought, helps bring a consideration of *Crime Wave* out of the limited milieu of the philosophy contemporaneous to its production. While adopting postmodern aesthetics, *Crime Wave* manages to transcend postmodern analyses and manifestos typical of its production context by anticipating critiques of postmodernism, such as Žižek's critique of the fundamental fantasies (e.g., possible freedom from master narratives) that underlie the postmodern politics of irony. Indeed, *Crime Wave* seems to embody, in its structure and subject, a critical position relative to the postmodern trappings of its own surface pastiche.

Wilden argues, in his essay on the "old question" of Canadian identity, that most Canadians around the time of *Crime Wave*'s production were "brought up to feel predominantly 'anti-American.' Others of us are trained to be 'pro-American.' Still others switch back and forth, at different times or at different levels, between the two opposed poles of this Imaginary relation ... A third position, however, transcends the dualism and one-dimensionality of the Imaginary relation ... This is a position and a perspective which allows us to take whatever we need from wherever we find it from whatever tradition ... and to transform them in whatever ways we find most fruitful and most useful."[18] To take and transform Wilden's next words, it is the position not of Canadian postmodernism, not of anti-American ironism, not of pro-Hollywood or pro-art-house or pro-paracinema anti-everything, but the position and the perspective of John Paizs's *Crime Wave*.

Production Credits

Director

John Paizs

Writer

John Paizs

Cast

(all significant speaking roles)

Eva Kovacs	Kim Brown
John Paizs	Steven Penny
Darrell Baran	Ronnie Boyles
Jeffrey Owen Madden	Skip Holliday
Tea Andrea Tanner	Dawn Holliday
Mark Hunter [Yuill]	Stanley Falco / "Sid"
Neil Lawrie	Dr C. Jolly / "Hank"
Bob Cloutier	Mr Brown
Donna Fillingham	Mrs Brown
Douglas Syms	Narrator

Producer

John Paizs

Original Music

Randolph Peters

Camera

John Paizs
Tom Fijal
Lorne Bailey (animation camera)

Editing

John Paizs
Gerry Klym
Jon Coutts

Art Department

John Paizs
Nick Burns

Set Decoration and Costume Design

Maria Paizs (costumes and draperies)

Makeup and Special Effects Department

Shawn Wilson (special make-up and effects)
Dave Peter (special make-up and effects)
Darren Bullerwell (effects assistant)

Sound Department

Gerry Klym (sound and sound effects)
Jon Stevens (sound)
Clive Perry (re-recording)
Conrad Tlatzkiw (sound effects)

Running Time

80 minutes

Aspect Ratio

1.33 : 1

Further Viewing

8½. Federico Fellini. 1963.

Adaptation. Spike Jonze. 2002.

Barton Fink. Joel and Ethan Coen. 1991.

Beginnings 1976–1983: The Early Years. Winnipeg Film Group. 2010. (Includes *The Obsession of Billy Botski*. John Paizs. 1980.)

Isolation in the 1980s. Winnipeg Film Group. 2005. (Includes *Springtime in Greenland*. John Paizs. 1981.)

Mulholland Dr. David Lynch. 2001.

Top of the Food Chain (a.k.a. *Invasion!*). John Paizs. 1999.

Notes

Epigraph

Jenny Boully, *The Book of Beginnings and Endings* (Louisville: Sarabande, 2007), 3.

Acknowledgments

1 Caelum Vatnsdal, *Kino Delirium: The Films of Guy Maddin* (Winnipeg: Arbeiter Ring, 2000), 13.

1. The Top! Few Films Made It!

1 Wikipedia, "*Crime Wave* (1985 film)." Available at http://en.wikipedia.org/wiki/Crime_Wave_(1985_film).
2 Geoff Pevere, "Dream On: The Crimes of John Paizs," *Place: 13 essays 13 filmmakers 1 city*, ed. Cecilia Araneda (Winnipeg: Winnipeg Film Group, 2009), 113.
3 Robert L. Cagle, "Persistence of Vision: The Wonderful World of John Paizs," *Cineaction* 57 (2002): 42.
4 Mark Peranson, "John Paizs Talks!", *Take One* 8.25 (1999): 22.
5 John Kozak, in curatorial notes for DVD collection, *Isolation in the 1980s* (Winnipeg: Winnipeg Film Group, 2005).
6 Will Straw, "Reinhabiting Lost Languages: Guy Maddin's *Careful*," *Play-*

ing with Memories: Essays on Guy Maddin, ed. David Church (Winnipeg: U of Manitoba P, 2009), 58.

7 Solomon Nagler, "Pre-Puberulent Inertia: Jeffrey Erbach and the Winnipeg Secession," *Place: 13 essays 13 filmmakers 1 city*, ed. Cecilia Araneda (Winnipeg: Winnipeg Film Group, 2009), 19.

8 Geoff Pevere, "Prairie Postmodern: An Introduction to the Mind & Films of John Paizs," *Cinema Canada* (1985): 11.

9 Peter Vesuwalla, "Paizs-ing the Way: Local Director's Masterpiece Opened the Door for Guy Maddin and Others," *Uptown* (2 February 2006): 25.

10 Bruce McDonald, interviewed in BRAVO, *On Screen!* episode devoted to *Crime Wave*, BRAVO, 16 March 2008.

11 Kozak, *Isolation in the 1980s*.

12 Pevere, "Dream On," 111.

13 Guy Maddin, "The Birth of a Mogul," *Midcontinental*, 11.

14 Marcus Boon, *In Praise of Copying* (Cambridge: Harvard UP, 2010), 71.

15 Fredric Jameson, "Postmodernism and Consumer Society," *The Cultural Turn: Selected Writings on the Postmodern, 1983–1998* (London: Verso, 1998), 4.

16 Ibid., 5.

17 Linda Hutcheon, *A Theory of Parody: The Teachings of Twentieth-Century Art Forms* (New York: Methuen, 1985), 33.

18 Ibid., 38.

19 Ibid., 34.

20 Boon, *In Praise of Copying*, 210.

21 Fredric Jameson, "Postmodernism, or The Cultural Logic of Late Capitalism," *New Left Review* 146 (July-August 1984): 20.

22 Jameson, "Postmodernism and Consumer Society," 20.

23 Boon, *In Praise of Copying*, 234.

24 Jean Baudrillard, *Simulations*, trans. Paul Foss, Paul Patton, and Philip Beitchman (New York: Semiotext[e], 1983), 40.

25 Peranson, "John Paizs Talks!", 22.

26 Linda Hutcheon, *Splitting Images: Contemporary Canadian Ironies* (Toronto: Oxford UP, 1991), 39.

27 Ibid., 17.

28 Ibid., 39.

29 Baudrillard, *Simulations*, 52.

30 Slavoj Žižek, *The Plague of Fantasies* (London: Verso, 1997), 30.
31 Hillel Schwartz, *The Culture of the Copy: Striking Likenesses, Unreasonable Facsimiles* (New York: Zone, 1996).
32 Boon, *In Praise of Copying*, 182.
33 Žižek, *The Plague of Fantasies*, 10.
34 Schwartz, *The Culture of the Copy*, 83.
35 Jean Baudrillard, *Fatal Strategies*, trans. Philippe Beitchman and W.G.J. Niesluchowski (New York: Semiotext[e], 2008), 152.
36 Žižek, *The Plague of Fantasies*, 121. As an example of how Žižek copies himself, the quoted passage and the paragraph within which it is embedded also appear in his *Organs without Bodies: Deleuze and Consequences* (New York: Routledge, 2004), 96. In the latter book, as is often the case in his writings, Žižek repeats the paragraph verbatim but begins to alter and expand his points near its end.
37 Ibid., 98.
38 Ibid., 66.
39 Straw, "Reinhabiting Lost Languages," 68.
40 Brian McHale, *Postmodernist Fiction* (New York: Methuen, 1987), xii.
41 Geoff Pevere, "John Paizs' *Crime Wave*," *Cinema Canada* (1986).
42 Ibid.
43 Straw, "Reinhabiting Lost Languages," 65.
44 Andrew Higson, "The Concept of a National Cinema," *Film and Nationalism*, ed. Alan Williams (Piscataway: Rutgers UP, 2002), 54.

2. Beginnings and Endings

1 Pevere, interviewed in BRAVO, *On Screen!*
2 Canuxploitation!, "Interview: John Paizs," *Canuxploitation!: Your Complete Guide to Canadian B-Film*. Available at http://canuxploitation.com/interview/paizs.html.
3 John Paizs, e-mail message to author, 20 July 2011.
4 Ibid.
5 Ibid.
6 Ibid.
7 Ibid.

8 Gene Walz, "Shack-Wacky Animation: The Case of Manitoba," *North of Everything: English-Canadian Cinema Since 1980*, eds. William Beard and Jerry White (Edmonton: U of Alberta P, 2002), 81.
9 John Paizs, e-mail message to author, 20 July 2011.
10 BRAVO, *On Screen!*
12 Maddin, qtd in Canadian Press NewsWire, "Movie Madness on the Prairies (Winnipeg Film Group)," (14 October 1994).
13 Patrick Lowe, in curatorial notes for DVD collection, *Beginnings 1976–1983: The Early Years* (Winnipeg: Winnipeg Film Group, 2010).
14 John Paizs, qtd in Nicolas Kazamia, "Exceptional Vistas: Quirky Cult Director John Paizs Is Back with His Screwball Sci-Fi movie, *Top of the Food Chain*," *National Post* (4 March 2000): 3.
15 Cagle, "Persistence of Vision," 45.
16 Ibid., 45.
17 Ibid., 45.
18 Ibid., 45.
19 Laura Mulvey, "Visual Pleasure and Narrative Cinema," *Film Theory and Criticism*, 5th ed., eds. Leo Braudy and Marshall Cohen (Oxford: Oxford UP, 1999), 842.
20 Ibid., 837.
21 Ibid., 836.
22 Cagle, "Persistence of Vision," 46.
23 BRAVO, *On Screen!*
24 McHale, *Postmodernist Fiction*, 30.
25 Ibid., 30.
26 Cagle, "Persistence of Vision," 46.
27 Ibid., 46.
28 Pevere, "Prairie Postmodern," 13.
29 Ibid., 13.
30 Ibid., 13.
31 Linda Hutcheon, "Irony, Nostalgia, and the Postmodern," University of Toronto English Library website (19 January 1998). Available at http://www.library.utoronto.ca/utel/criticism/hutchinp.html.
32 Steven Connor, *Postmodernist Culture*, 2nd ed. (Oxford: Blackwell, 1997), 45.
33 Hutcheon, "Irony, Nostalgia, and the Postmodern."

34 Cagle, "Persistence of Vision," 48.
35 Ibid., 48.
36 Pevere, "Prairie Postmodern," 13.
37 Cagle, "Persistence of Vision," 48.
38 Ibid., 48.
39 Ibid., 48.
40 Ibid., 48.
41 McHale, *Postmodernist Fiction*, 11.
42 Ibid., 11.
43 Pevere, "Dream On," 108.
44 Ibid., 108.
45 Canuxploitation!, "Interview: John Paizs."
46 John Paizs, e-mail message to author, 6 July 2011.
47 Pevere, "Dream On," 112.
48 Ibid., 112.
49 John Paizs, e-mail message to author, 6 July 2011.
50 John Paizs, e-mail message to author, 20 July 2011.
51 Jay Scott, "Half-Cooked Crime Wave: Winnipeg Director Can't Quite End It All," *Globe and Mail* (14 September 1985).
52 Ibid.
53 John Paizs, e-mail message to author, 6 July 2011.
54 Ibid.
55 Klymkiw, interviewed in BRAVO, *On Screen!*
56 John Paizs, e-mail message to author, 6 July 2011.
57 Morley Walker, "Raves for Wave: *Crime Wave* Vaults Winnipegger into Big Time," *Winnipeg Sun* (3 October 1985).
58 Qtd. in ibid.
59 Tom McSorley, "The Beginnings of the Beginnings: Canada's Top 10 Fiction Feature Film Debuts Since 1968," *Take One* (December 2003–March 2004), 31.
60 Alex Grant, "Paizs' Film Noir Parody *Crime Wave* Invited to Vancouver In New Form,' in *Variety* (7 May 1986).
61 Greg McIntyre, "Theft Disrupts *Crime Wave*," *The Province* (23 March 1986): 5.
62 Stephanie Ostick, "City Man's Film Ready for Release," *Winnipeg Free Press* (18 December 1986).
63 Ibid.

64 Geoffrey York, "Waiting It Out in Winnipeg," *Globe and Mail* (29 or 30? January 1987), D1.
65 Canadian Press, "Sale of Alliance Films to eOne for $225 million completed," *CTV News* (9 January 2013). Available at http://www.ctvnews.ca/entertainment/sale-of-alliance-films-to-eone-for-225-million-completed-1.1106510.
66 John Paizs, e-mail message to author, 20 July 2011.
67 Ibid.
68 Ibid.
69 John Paizs, e-mail message to author, 6 July 2011.
70 Ibid.
71 John Paizs, e-mail message to author, 20 July 2011.
72 Paizs qtd in Kazamia, "Exceptional Vistas," 3.
73 Canuxploitation!, "Interview: John Paizs."
74 Not Coming to a Theatre Near You, "An Interview with John Paizs." Available at http://www.notcoming.com/features/johnpaizsinterview.
75 Canuxploitation!, "Interview: John Paizs."

3. The Greatest Color Crime Movie Never Made

1 Jeffrey Sconce, "'Trashing' the Academy: Taste, Excess, and an Emerging Politics of Cinematic Style," *Screen* 36.4 (1995): 371–93.
2 John Paizs, e-mail message to author, 25 September 2012.
3 Not Coming to a Theatre Near You, "An Interview with John Paizs."
4 BRAVO, *On Screen!*
5 John Paizs, e-mail messages to author, 1–2 June 2012.
6 Ibid.
7 Ibid.
8 Ibid.
9 John Paizs, e-mail message to author, 25 September 2012.
10 Christopher Harris, "*Crime Wave*'s Insanity Satirizes Pop Culture," *Ottawa Citizen* (25 October 1985): F22.
11 John Paizs, "Crime Wave" (typewritten screenplay, 1984, from the personal collection of John Paizs).
12 Žižek, *The Plague of Fantasies*, 119.

13 Andrew Gibson, *Towards a Postmodern Theory of Narrative* (Edinburgh: Edinburgh UP, 1996), 234.
14 John Paizs, e-mail message to author, 20 July 2011.
15 John Paizs, e-mail message to author, 25 September 2012.
16 Ibid.
17 Jamie Portman, "A Young Winnipeg Film-Maker Is Riding High," Southam News (21 May 1987): 1.
18 John Paizs, e-mail message to author, 25 September 2012.
19 BRAVO, *On Screen!*
20 Eva Kovacs, qtd in Randall King, "A Life of Crime," *Winnipeg Free Press* (28 January 2006).
21 Zoë Druick, *Allan King's "A Married Couple"* (Toronto: U of Toronto P, 2010), 74.
22 Mary Ann Doane, "The Voice in the Cinema: The Articulation of Body and Space," *Film Theory and Criticism*, 5th ed., eds. Leo Braudy and Marshall Cohen (Oxford: Oxford UP, 1999), 372.
23 John Paizs, e-mail message to author, 25 September 2012.
24 Peter Wollen, "Godard and Counter Cinema: *Vent D'Est*," *Film Theory and Criticism*, 5th ed., eds. Leo Braudy and Marshall Cohen (Oxford: Oxford UP, 1999), 504.
25 John Paizs, e-mail message to author, 24 September 2012.
26 Ibid.
27 Pevere interviewed in BRAVO, *On Screen!*
28 John Paizs, e-mail message to author, 25 September 2012.
29 Ibid.
30 John Paizs, e-mail message to author, 24 September 2012.
31 John Paizs, e-mail message to author, 25 September 2012.
32 House of Self-Indulgence, review of *Crime Wave* (29 January 2010). Available at http://houseofselfindulgence.blogspot.com/2010/01/crime-wave-john-paizs-1985.html.
33 BRAVO, *On Screen!*
34 Cagle, "Persistence of Vision," 49.
35 John Paizs, "Crime Wave" (rewritten screenplay ending, [1985], from the personal collection of John Paizs), 9.
36 Ibid., 10.

37 Paizs, "Crime Wave" (typewritten screenplay), 7.
38 Ibid., 7.
39 Ibid., 7.
40 Ibid., 8.
41 Ibid., 8.
42 Ibid., 8.
43 Ibid., 8.
44 Ibid., 8.
45 Bart Beaty, *David Cronenberg's "A History of Violence"* (Toronto: U of Toronto P, 2008), 41.
46 Paizs, "Crime Wave" (typewritten screenplay), 10.
47 John Paizs, "Crime Wave" (handwritten screenplay, [1984], from the personal collection of John Paizs), n.pag.
48 John Paizs, e-mail message to author, 25 September 2012.
49 John Paizs, in Jason Anderson, *Eye Weekly* interview (2008). Available at http://www.eyeweekly.com/print/article/23758.
50 John Paizs, e-mail message to author, 25 September 2012.
51 John Paizs, e-mail message to author, 6 July 2011.
52 Ibid.
53 John Paizs, e-mail message to author, 25 September 2012.
54 Paizs, "Crime Wave" (handwritten screenplay), n.pag.
55 John Paizs, e-mail message to author, 6 July 2011.
56 Ibid.
57 Milan Kundera, *The Art of the Novel* (New York: HarperCollins, 2000 [1986]), 26.
58 Paizs, "Crime Wave" (typewritten screenplay), 15.
59 Ibid., 15.

4. The Stuff In-Between

1 John Paizs, e-mail message to author, 25 September 2012.
2 Ibid.
3 Ibid.
4 John Paizs, e-mail message to author, 27 September 2012.
5 Paizs, "Crime Wave" (typewritten screenplay), 20.

6 Geoff Pevere, "Guy Maddin: True to Form," *Playing with Memories: Essays on Guy Maddin*, ed. David Church (Winnipeg: U of Manitoba P, 2009), 52.
7 Paizs, "Crime Wave" (handwritten screenplay), n.pag.
8 Ibid., n.pag.
9 Ibid., n.pag.
10 Ibid., n.pag.
11 Sconce, "'Trashing' the Academy," 372.
12 Lowe, *Beginnings 1976–1983*, n.pag.
13 David Kronke, "Paizs parodies '50s naivete," *Times Herald*, ca. 1985–6.
14 Peranson, "John Paizs Talks!," 22.
15 Cagle, "Persistence of Vision, 49.
16 Not Coming to a Theatre Near You, "An Interview with John Paizs."
17 Žižek, *The Plague of Fantasies*, 122.
18 Bruce Fink, *The Lacanian Subject: Between Language and Jouissance* (Princeton: Princeton UP, 1995), 52.

5. Twists!

1 John Paizs, e-mail message to author, 25 September 2012.
2 Paizs, "Crime Wave" (typewritten screenplay), 28–9.
3 Ibid., 29.
4 Scott, "Half-Cooked Crime Wave."
5 Todd McGowan, *The Impossible David Lynch* (New York: Columbia UP, 2007), 12–13.
6 Ibid., 20.
7 Pevere, *Cinema Canada* review.
8 John Paizs, e-mail message to author, 24 September 2012.
9 Ibid.
10 Ibid.
11 Nagler, "Pre-Puberulent Inertia," 20.
12 Kronke, "Paizs parodies '50s naivete."
13 Peranson, "John Paizs Talks!," 22.
14 Ibid., 22.
15 Not Coming to a Theatre Near You, "An Interview with John Paizs."

16 John Paizs, e-mail message to author, 25 September 2012.
17 Ibid.
18 Ibid.

6. The Gap Exposing the Real

1 Sigmund Freud, "The 'Uncanny,'" *The Standard Edition of the Complete Psychological Works of Sigmund Freud, Volume XVII (1917–1919): An Infantile Neurosis and Other Works* (London: Hogarth, 1991), 235.
2 John Paizs, "Crime Wave" (rewritten screenplay ending, [1985], from the personal collection of John Paizs), 5.
3 Ibid., 5.
4 Ibid., 5.
5 Klymkiw interviewed in BRAVO, *On Screen!*
6 Fredric Jameson, *The Geopolitical Aesthetic: Cinema and Space in the World System* (Bloomington: Indiana UP, 1992), 84n19.
7 John Paizs, e-mail message to author, 25 September 2012.
8 Paizs interviewed in BRAVO, *On Screen!*
9 Paizs, "Crime Wave" (rewritten screenplay ending), 7.
10 Ibid., 8–9.
11 John Paizs, e-mail message to author, 25 September 2012.
12 Ibid.
13 Žižek, *The Plague of Fantasies*, 141.
14 Ibid., 15.
15 Ibid., 40n6.
16 Paizs, "Crime Wave" (rewritten screenplay ending), 10-11.
17 Žižek, *The Plague of Fantasies*, 142.

7. An Alternate Universe

1 Pevere, "Dream On," 112.
2 Scott, "Half-Cooked Crime Wave."
3 Slavoj Žižek, *Welcome to the Desert of the Real* (New York: Verso, 2002), 70–1.
4 Skizz Cyzyk, "Tragically Obscure: John Paizs' *(The Big) Crimewave*,' in *Cashiers du Cinemart* 9. Available at http://www.impossiblefunky.com.

8. From the North

1 Tom McSorley, *Atom Egoyan's The Adjuster* (Toronto: U of Toronto P, 2009), 61.
2 Fredric Jameson, "Foreword," *Canadian Cultural Studies: A Reader*, eds. Sourayan Mookerjea, Imre Szeman, and Gail Faurschou (Durham: Duke UP, 2009), xii.
3 Anthony Wilden, "The Old Question, but Not the Old Answers," *Canadian Cultural Studies: A Reader*, eds. Sourayan Mookerjea, Imre Szeman, and Gail Faurschou (Durham: Duke UP, 2009), 212.
4 Ibid., 223.
5 Hutcheon, *Splitting Images*, 36.
6 Pevere, "Dream On," 108.
7 Matthew Rankin, qtd in Darren Wershler, *Guy Maddin's My Winnipeg* (Toronto: U of Toronto P, 2010), 66.
8 Hutcheon, *Splitting Images*, vii.
9 Pevere, "Prairie Postmodern," 13.
10 Pevere, *Cinema Canada* review.
11 Peranson, "John Paizs Talks!," 22.
12 Pevere, "Dream On," 113.
13 Pevere, *Cinema Canada* review.
14 Peranson, "John Paizs Talks!," 22
15 Maddin, "The Birth of a Mogul," 11.
16 Pevere, "Prairie Postmodern," 13.
17 Hutcheon, *Splitting Images*, 3.
18 Wilden, "The Old Question, but Not the Old Answers," 224.

Selected Bibliography

On John Paizs

Cagle, Robert L. "Persistence of Vision: The Wonderful World of John Paizs." *Cineaction* 57 (2002): 42–8.

Cyzyk, Skizz. "Then from the North ... Or, My Weekend with John Paizs." *Cashiers du Cinemart* 10. Available at http://www.impossiblefunky.com.

Kazamia, Nicolas. "Exceptional Vistas: Quirky Cult Director John Paizs Is Back with His Screwball Sci-Fi Movie, *Top of the Food Chain*." *National Post* (4 March 2000): 3.

Maddin, Guy. "The Birth of a Mogul." *Midcontinental*: 10–11.

Peranson, Mark. "John Paizs Talks!" *Take One* 8.25 (1999): 22.

Peary, Gerald. "Crime Paizs." *Flare* (February 1986): 75, 77.

Pevere, Geoff. "Dream On: The Crimes of John Paizs." *Place: 13 essays 13 filmmakers 1 city*. Ed. Cecilia Araneda. Winnipeg: Winnipeg Film Group, 2009. 106–13.

– "Prairie Postmodern: An Introduction to the Mind & Films of John Paizs." *Cinema Canada* (April 1985): 11–13.

York, Geoffrey. "Waiting It Out in Winnipeg." *Globe and Mail* (30 January 1987): D1.

Reviews of *Crime Wave*

Brauer, David. "Crime Time." *Twin Cities Reader* (25 March 1987).

Cyzyk, Skizz. "Tragically Obscure: John Paizs' *(The Big) Crimewave*." *Cashiers du Cinemart* 9. Available at http://www.impossiblefunky.com.

Grant, Alex. "Paizs' Film Noir Parody *Crime Wave* Invited to Vancouver in New Form." *Variety* (7 May 1986).

King, Randall. "A Life of Crime." *Winnipeg Free Press,* 28 January 2006).

Kronke, David. "Paizs Parodies '50s Naivete." *Times Herald.*

Nakhnikian, Elise. "A Movie a Day, Day 42: *Crime Wave.*" *Slant* (27 June 2010). Available at http://www.slantmagazine.com/house/2010/06/a-movie-a-day-day-42-crime-wave.

Pevere, Geoff. "John Paizs' *Crime Wave.*" *Cinema Canada* (1986).

Scott, Jay. "Half-Cooked Crime Wave: Winnipeg Director Can't Quite End It All." *Globe and Mail* (14 September 1985).

Vesuwalla, Peter. "Paizs-ing the Way: Local Director's Masterpiece Opened the Door for Guy Maddin and Others." *Uptown* (2 February 2006): 25.

CANADIAN CINEMA

Edited by Bart Beaty and Will Straw

1 Bart Beaty. *David Cronenberg's "A History of Violence"*
2 André Loiselle. *Denys Arcand's "Le Déclin de l'empire américain" and "Les Invasions barbares"*
3 Tom McSorley. *Atom Egoyan's "The Adjuster"*
4 Johanne Sloan. *Joyce Wieland's "The Far Shore"*
5 Zoë Druick. *Allan King's "A Married Couple"*
6 Darren Wershler. *Guy Maddin's "My Winnipeg"*
7 Paul McEwan. *Bruce McDonald's "Hard Core Logo"*
8 Geoff Pevere. *Don Shebib's "Goin' Down the Road"*
9 Darrell Varga. *John Walker's "Passage"*
10 Ernest Mathijs. *John Fawcett's "Ginger Snaps"*
11 Jonathan Ball. *John Paizs's "Crime Wave"*

www.ingramcontent.com/pod-product-compliance
Lightning Source LLC
Chambersburg PA
CBHW020454260925
33189CB00001B/95
* 9 7 8 1 4 4 2 6 1 6 1 7 2 *